Christian Thought

Study Guide

New Specification OCR H573/3

Peter Baron & Daniella Dunsmore

Contents

Introduction

Some Uniting Questions

There are four questions that give unity to this paper and indeed, to the whole specification.

1. What does it mean to be human? The secular Darwinist worldview sees human beings as a highly intelligent, well adapted animal. But Augustine, Aquinas, Calvin, Bonhoeffer all see human beings as in some sense made in the image of God - **imago dei** in Latin. We need to be clear that something is lost if we reduce human beings to higher order animals - the issue is, what is lost, and does it matter?

    In 1941 Bishop Galen of Munster delivered a stinging rebuke to Nazi leaders for their programme of murdering, by non-voluntary euthanasia, people considered to have 'lives not worthy of life' (such as the mentally subnormal and handicapped). His words are worth reading:

    According to the information I have received it is planned in the course of this week to move a large number of inmates of the provincial hospital at Marienthal, classified as "unproductive members of the national community," to the mental hospital at Eichberg, where, they are to be deliberately killed. Since such action is not only contrary to the divine and the natural moral law but under article 211 of the German Penal Code ranks as murder and attracts the death penalty, I hereby report the matter in accordance with my obligation under article 139 of the Penal Code and request that steps should at once be taken to protect the patients concerned by proceedings against the authorities planning their removal and murder, and that I may be informed of the action taken. (Bishop Galen, sermon preached in Munster, 1941).

    Before we are tempted to feel morally superior, note how the US state of Indiana imposed forced sterilisation on 'imbeciles and mentally subnormals' in legislation dated 1907. Over 30 states followed suit, continuing the practice in some cases up until the 1960s. Over 65,000 individuals were forcibly sterilised in 33 American states.

    To be human here meant a higher form of rational being and a genetic grading of fellow citizens. Those who didn't fit this definition of genetic purity were not allowed to have children. The Levitical purity code reinvented itself in genetics and eugenics and became an ugly deformation of our understanding of what it means to be fully human.

How crucial, then to keep this question to the forefront of our minds - what does it mean to be human, and in what ways are sections of our own society, or nations of our world, being dehumanised even as I write this?

2. What are the origins of good and evil? Augustine traces evil to the Fall of Humankind in Genesis 3 - what is sometimes called 'man's first disobedience'. Calvin in the sixteenth century agrees. But to Freud and Dawkins, two secular thinkers, good and evil are either psychological manifestations of human guilt which are essentially induced in us by our upbringing (Freud) or it is part of our evolved natures as co-operative animals (Dawkins) which has yielded an 'altruistic gene'. What part does our Christian heritage play in forming our present self-perception?

3. What is the place of metaphysics in our worldview? Metaphysics (that which means 'beyond physics') is bigger than the God-concept alone - it includes questions of beauty, truth and meaning which atheist and believer alike can recognise. After all love is a metaphysical idea. Does metaphysics make more sense with God, or without God? The fact that most people today classify themselves as having 'no religion' (2016 survey) does not mean that they have 'no faith'. Indeed Alister McGrath argues that natural theology helps give us a holistic **fiduciary framework** (faith-based) - and even Dawkins has a fiduciary framework which he rarely acknowledges.

4. How has the version of Christianity changed over time? Alasdair MacIntyre once observed 'the Christianity most people disbelieve in is a product of the last three hundred years'. In other words, it's a reaction to the Enlightenment project, which included not just the enthronement of the empirical, but the dethronement of metaphysics. Theologians used natural theology (such as the design argument) to try to prove God exists. Evangelical Christians tried to prove the Bible is infallible and inerrant (without mistakes). Meantime prophetic movements arose in Latin America preaching liberation of the oppressed, and feminist theologians led a severe criticism of the patriarchal, male god-figure. As culture fragmented into postmodernity, so new Christianities arose to reinvigorate old versions or even reject them altogether. Consider the table on the facing page.

Taking some of the key thinkers named by the specification and placing them into eras of history we can see the following stages are considered.

Era	Philosophy of Religion H573/1	Ethics H573/2	Christian Thought H573/3
Ancient	Plato, Aristotle	Aristotle	Plato, Arsitotle
Early Christian	Augustine, Irenaeus, Boethius		Augustine
Medieval	Anselm, Aquinas	Aquinas (Natural Law & Conscience)	Aquinas
Enlightenment	Kant Hume	Kant Utilitarians Hume	Calvin Kant Hume
Modern	Ayer Wittgenstein Malcolm Swinburne Hare Mitchell Hick	Fletcher Ayer Wittgenstein Freud (Conscience)	Hick (Pluralism) Dawkins (Secularism) Freud (Secularism)

Ideas do not appear in a vacuum but emerge from stages of history, or world-views. These views are not static but go through stages of evolution, until a moment arrives for what Thomas Kuhn calls a 'paradigm shift'.

Examples of paradigm shifts include:

1. The Copernican Revolution of the fifteenth and sixteenth centuries saw a fundamental change of perspective as the world was no longer at the centre with the stars orbiting round it, but based on observation, the sun was established as the centre.

2. The Reformation which began with Martin Luther's nailing of ninety-five theses on the door of a church in Wittenberg in 1517 created an idea of the individual at the centre of our relationship with God, and the authority of the Church was thereby diminished. Scripture and reason became paramount, but by elevating reason and the individual the Reformation also created an environment of thinking where human rights and equality came to the forefront of the agenda - in a sense sowing the seeds of religion's own demise.

3. Darwin's revolution, beginning with the publication of the Origin of Species in 1863, challenged theological understandings of the origin of the world and the uniqueness of humans. We were not

God-created but naturally-evolved extensions of the animal kingdom. Darwinism is studied in the secularism section of the Christian Thought paper which considers Darwinism and Richard Dawkins' attack on religion and faith, but it is also relevant to the teleological arguments of thinkers like William Paley, who infer purpose from patterns and design. For Dawkins there is no purpose in nature.

4. Finally the Psychological revolution, that began with Freud, fundamentally reinterprets what it means to be human, and the place of human responsibility and the concept of human sin. "Sin" becomes behaviour which we cannot accept according to prevailing norms, which are to be explained in terms of subconscious forces, such as repressed desires for a mother or father figure. Just as Freud interprets sin as socially unacceptable behaviour which can be explained by psychological drives, so the liberation theologians also fundamentally reinterpret sin as structural - coming from material facts of life, such as power relations reflected in property ownership and ownership of the means of production. Sin for a liberationist means unjust praxis.

The phrase 'paradigm shift' implies an instant revolution - but of course in practice new ideas take time (decades) to change the fundamental foundation world-view. Arguably we still live with vestiges of all world-views - for example, the fundamentalist version of Islam we find in the terrorist organisation ISIS is really a medieval mindset where death is visited on the idolater and blasphemer, the attitudes to women are barbarous, and the idea of the divine will and divine rewards primitive. It is exactly how Christians behaved to Muslims, and to each other, in the medieval period.

Notice also that something produces the shift and that arguably the big shift from the Greek worldview to the early Christian worldview is produced by the decisive entry of God into the world - in the incarnation of Jesus Christ - or at least, even an atheist might concede, the influence of Christianity on the development of world-views is an important and foundational question.

It is interesting, though, to consider whether the Jesus movement was actually a Jewish reform movement or a radical break. The Jewish author Gaza Vermes has interesting insights into this question. Reversing this argument we can also see that John's gospel, written late in about AD90 is profoundly Greek in its ideas, with Jesus described as the Logos or divine word become flesh (John 1). Did Christianity influence philosophy, or philosophy influence Christianity? Feminist theologians such as Rosemary Ruether invoke the idea of Jesus as the genderless divine wisdom or Logos, showing a bias in favour of John's interpretation of the Christ-event.

An Underlying Integrating Principle - Hermeneutics

Hermeneutics means 'the study of interpretation' after Hermes who was messenger (interpreter) to the gods. The issue that underlies our specification is: how has the idea of God been interpreted over time and by different cultures?

Does this explain the many varieties of Christianity we see in the world today, and the every different varieties in history - some very violent (the Crusaders), some pacifist (the Quakers), some quite radically prophetic (The Montanists), some world-renouncing (Monasticism), some ecologically friendly (Franciscans).

Hans-Georg Gadamer describes this contrast between ourselves and a distant culture or text as the 'two horizons' of hermeneutics. Professor Anthony Thiselton explains the metaphor of 'horizon' in this way:

The goal of biblical hermeneutics is to bring about an active and meaningful engagement between the interpreter and text, in such a way that the interpreter's own horizon is re-shaped and enlarged. In one sense it is possible to speak, with Gadamer, of the goal of hermeneutics as a "fusion" of horizons. In practice, because the interpreter cannot leap out of the historical tradition to which he belongs, the two horizons can never become totally identical; at best they remain separate but close. Nevertheless the problem of historical distance and tradition should not give rise to undue pessimism. Even if the problems of hermeneutics are not trivial, neither are they insoluble, and there is always progress towards a fusion of horizons. The Bible can and does speak today, in such a way as to correct, reshape, and enlarge the interpreter's own horizons. (The Two Horizons of Hermeneutics, page xix).

We tend to read the Bible and any ancient text from the perspective of our own time. In this way the Bible continues to live today in real applications. The Liberation theologian shares with the feminist theologian a discerning of a golden thread of a prophetic-liberating tradition. Passages such as the Exodus are taken as describing the liberator God who intervenes to save his people from the appalling state of slavery in Egypt. The oppressors are judged by the miracle of the opening and closing of the waters, so that the pursuing armies of Pharaoh drown before they can attack the Israelites., swallowed up in a hell of water as the Red Sea closes in.

In a later chapter I consider how we should treat the passages which are listed in our specification (there are eleven in total that could feature in an exam question on Christian Thought, and only two of these are from the Old Testament, Genesis 3 and Exodus 20). One excellent way to start the course in Year 1 is to examine carefully Genesis 3 (Augustine and Human Nature section) and a New Testament parable such as Matthew 25, the parable of The Sheep and The Goats (Death and the Afterlife section), first from a reader-response perspective (just read it 'raw' and ask students to comment on the text and find resonances today, or in their own immediate experience) and then read the interpretations in history, for example, in Augustine or Aquinas or Calvin, or in modern times, from a feminist and a conservative evangelical perspective.

Just seeing the variety of interpretations shows how Gadamer's task of fusing horizons is worked out in practice. In this process, try taking a radically new translation of the Bible such as The Message, which will help you really hear what it is saying. Familiarity breeds deafness when it comes to Bible stories.

Many of the debates in today's church (for example, in sexual ethics, or the place of women in the church, based on a text such as Ephesians 5:21-33 which is part of our specification under Gender and Society) are debates about hermeneutics, and which principles we may or may not bring to bear in interpreting bible texts.

None of us, however, are entirely free from prejudice and preconception - and the claim to pure readings of Scripture (both Catholic, invoking natural law and arguing homosexuality is 'intrinsically disordered, or some varieties of Protestantism, which invokes ideas of biblical inerrancy and infallibility) is really a form of power play, saying in effect 'accept my interpretation, or you'll be damned', or in Roman Catholic terms, excommunicated.

Of course, that is hardly the grounds for damnation given by Jesus in his parable in Matthew 25 - which suggests that it's whether we treat the poor and the outcast as if treating Jesus himself that will be the grounds for division between saved and damned.

What you do to the least of these you do also to me, (Matthew 25:40)

Exercise: Research Interpretations of Genesis 3 given by Augustine and Aquinas. How and why do you think interpretations such of these have changed?

Augustine's Teaching on Human Nature

Structure of Thought

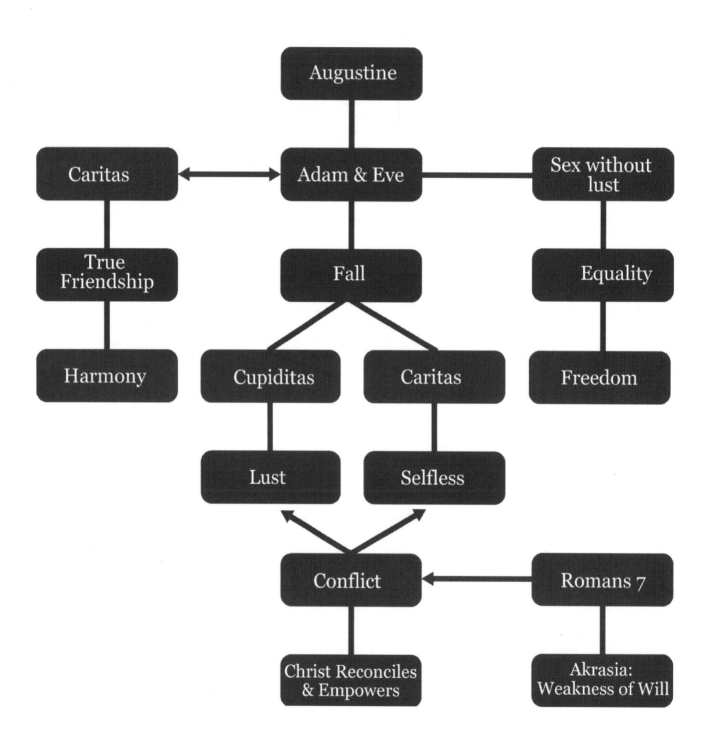

Augustine's Teaching on Human Nature

Human Relationships pre- and post-Fall

Augustine's Interpretation of Genesis 3

Before the Fall, Augustine asserts that there was harmony (concordia). Adam and Eve lived in obedience to God and had duties of stewardship to the other created animals. Augustine suggests that the human will, the body, and reason cooperated fully with each other.

Exercise: Identify quotations from Genesis 3 that support the claims made below.

- Adam and Eve live freely in the garden and are clear on God's instructions.

- Adam and Eve live in friendship, 'sharing' rather than taking from each other

- The blame of deception begins when God meets them and asks 'what are you doing here?". Disharmony arises after the first disobedience.

- Punishments are aligned with male and female biological sexual natures.

The State of Perfection before the Fall

Adam and Eve were married in a state of friendship (caritas) that included sex but not lust:

"Then (had there been no sin) the man would have sowed the seed and woman would have conceived the child when their sexual organs had been aroused by the will, at the appropriate time and in the necessary degree, and had not been excited by lust" Augustine, *City of God, Book 14, Chapter 24*

Adam and Eve did not realise their nakedness until after the Fall and so sex pre-Fall would have been without lust and instead, could be achieved at will.

Lust and Selfish Desires after the Fall

Adam and Eve's recognition of their sexual bodies is forever linked with their first disobedience. Cupiditas (lust) enters human experience.

"For they would not have arrived at the evil act if an evil will had not preceded it, Now, could anything but pride have been the start of the evil will? For 'pride is the start of every kind of sin'. And what is pride except for a perverse kind of exaltation?" Augustine, City of God, Book 4, Chapter 13.

Exercise: Analyse the extract from Augustine above. He says that an evil will must have preceded the evil act and that this was a will that came from pride. How could this be if Adam and Eve truly existed in harmony pre-Fall? Can pride be part of a harmonious world?

Original Sin and its Effects on the Will and Human Societies

Augustine's teaching that Original Sin is passed on through sexual intercourse and is the cause of human selfishness and lack of free will.

Post-Fall, the will is divided. It can recognise goodness but is motivated by desire rather than by love or goodness. In conflict with itself, the will is unable to obey itself. **Akrasia** (weakness of will) describes the paradox of choosing to do that which goes against our best interests.

Exercise: Define caritas, concupiscence, Concordia and akrasia. Explain how each relates to the state of human nature pre- and post-Fall.

Exercise: Consider the extract from Romans 7 (St Paul) below. How is akrasia (weakness of will) shown?

I do not understand what I do. For what I want to do I do not do, but what I hate I do. ₁₆ And if I do what I do not want to do, I agree that the law is good. ₁₇ As it is, it is no longer I myself who do it, but it is sin living in me. ₁₈ For I know that good itself does not dwell in me, that is, in my sinful nature. For I have the desire to do what is good, but I cannot carry it out. ₁₉ For I do not do the good I want to do, but the evil I do not want to do—this I keep on doing. ₂₀ Now if I do what I do not want to do, it is no longer I who do it, but it is sin living in me that does it. ₂₁ So I find this law at work: Although I want to do good, evil is right there with me. ₂₂ For in my inner being I delight in God's law; ₂₃ but I see another law at work in me, waging war against the law of my mind and making me a prisoner of the law of sin at work within me. 24 What a wretched man I am! Who will rescue me from this body that is subject to death? (Romans 7:15-24)

Augustine also echoes this paradoxical state of the will, shown in Confessions:

11. Thus came I to understand, from my own experience, what I had read, how that the flesh lusts against the Spirit, and the Spirit against the flesh. (Galatians 5:17) I verily lusted both ways; yet more in that which I approved in myself, than in that which I disapproved in myself. For in this last it was now rather not I, (Romans 7:20) because in much I rather suffered against my will than did it willingly. (Augustine, Confessions, 11)

Here, Augustine describes the domination of lust over the soul and the will. These uncontrolled desires mean that the body craves power, money, food and sex and seriously affects friendships. Augustine's example of a beautiful chaste woman who cannot convince him to be celibate shows the will at war with itself.

Exercise: Consider the following sentences from a commentary on Paul's letter to Romans. Find a quotation from the Pauline extract above to match each of the statements:

• Paul's problem is not a lack of desire. He wants to do what is right.

• Paul recognises that in sinning, he acts against his own nature.

• The 'real self' delights in God's will.

• Sin wins the battle of 'self' as there is no power within man to win.

- One must reach a state of complete desperation to reach victory.

- Paul looks outside of himself and his own self-focus that had previously dominated.

- He turns to Jesus.

Lack of Stability and Corruption in all Human Societies

Sin as an Ontological Condition

Augustine said sin was part of the essence (ontology = essence) of being human. Virtue is an appearance but we are not, by nature, good. Sexual intercourse provides the channel for original sin to be passed on. This seminal passing on of sin causes human selfishness and a lack of free will; and a lack of stability and corruption in all human societies.

For Augustine, Adam's successors shared in a collective alienation' and so unbaptised babies were also condemned. This was a view criticised by Pelagians.

Exercise: Define pre-Lapsarian, post-Lapsarian, ontological

Exercise: Re-read John 3. How might this have led Augustine to believe that anyone deliberately denying baptism could not reach Heaven?

Thought Point (Connections)

- Freud argues there is a conflict between eros (life-instinct) and Thanatos (death instinct) in the Id. This echoes Paul's argument in Romans 7 – Christ delivers us from 'this body of death'.

- Plato's charioteer analogy sees reason struggling to control the twin forces of nobler emotion (like courage) and passions or cravings which are on conflict.

Criticisms of Augustine

Julian, Bishop of Eclanum (386-455), disagreed with Augustine's language describing sex as a transmitter of sin. Julian was a Pelagian and thought Augustine's pessimism showed a hated of God's creation. Augustine seems to deny that God's giving of free will to humans allowed them to stand independently.

Is sin is transmitted through sex, then even through marriage, sex is tainted.

Augustine's Defence

All humans experience sex as a source of tension – personal or social. Humans are different to animals – sex remains private, even within marriage and sexual urges are a source of continual danger, rather than emerging at certain mating seasons throughout the year.

The body and will can be in conflict with the body willing but the will and reason uncertain. Augustine uses these points to argue that the Fall did not bring about sex, but rather, affected it. Pre-Fall, sex was under control of the will. Although nuns and monks had chosen the 'higher life', Christian marriage should not be ridiculed – physical delight in marriage is different to libido and the three goods of procreation, mutual fidelity and indissolubility should be respected. Still, there is 'nothing more beautiful than the sexless friendship of the elderly'.

Exercise: How does Augustine's view of free will change between books 1, 2 and 3 of Confessions? Clue – some might say it becomes more pessimistic.

On the nature of men and women, Augustine is sometimes seen as being more sympathetic to women than his contemporaries. He claimed men and women were created equal but different with their different roles being determined by their bodies. The argument that woman being made out of man's rib makes her subservient did not sit well with Augustine.

Instead, he said, this indicated their shared spiritual nature. Women were subordinate rationally but not spiritually – otherwise they would not be able to know God and be saved.

Exercise: How are Augustine's views visible in Catholic teaching today?

"An act of mutual love which impairs the capacity to transmit life . . . contradicts the will of the Author of life." We acknowledge God's design by "respecting the laws of conception, "which allows us to be "the minister of the design established by the Creator." Therefore, artificial birth control, sterilization, and abortion "are to be absolutely excluded as lawful means of regulating the number of children." (Humanae Vitae) A Summary of Pope Paul VI's Prophetic Encyclical, Scott Richert

God's Grace

Augustine's teaching that only God's grace, his generous love, can overcome sin and the rebellious will to achieve the greatest good (summum bonum).

Augustine taught that only God's grace could overcome the rebellious will. The Christian doctrine of election teaches that salvation is possible because God first chooses to redeem humans. God elects those he knows will freely answer his love and be restored to paradise and these elect are aided by the Holy Spirit.

Exercise: Create a diagram showing Augustine's thoughts on the human will pre- and post- Fall Augustine disagreed with the Greek theological belief in election being based on foreseen merits of individuals. Augustine did not agree that God's election could be caused by the past, present or future action of mankind. Human knowledge does not include that of our own election.

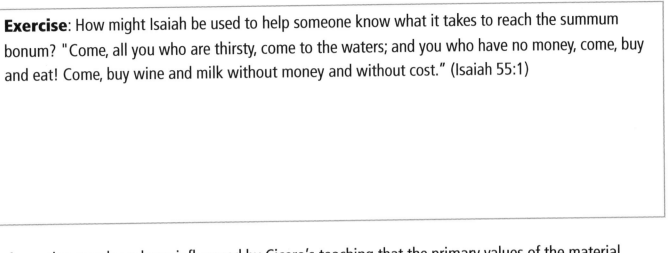

Exercise: How might Isaiah be used to help someone know what it takes to reach the summmum bonum? "Come, all you who are thirsty, come to the waters; and you who have no money, come, buy and eat! Come, buy wine and milk without money and without cost." (Isaiah 55:1)

Augustine may have been influenced by Cicero's teaching that the primary values of the material world – money, honour and sex, cannot pave the way to happiness – neither for society nor for the individual.

The Challenge of the Humanitarian Principle

This proposes that humans get on better when each rational person considers the rational interests of others. The focus on human reason rather than God being the source of knowledge was post-enlightenment thought with Hume and Kant taking a lead. Dawkins and Pinker furthered ideas to speak of the dangers of religion. For them, the humanitarian principle replaces the irrational superstitions of Original Sin, redemption, Grace and the Fall.

We can succeed without God's grace as our autonomous reasoning is enough.

Exercise: Assess the strengths and weaknesses of the challenge posed by the humanitarian principle.

Four Challenges to Augustine

1. Evolutionary biology is the framework for Dawkins' criticism that the doctrine of Original Sin is 'absurd and dangerous'. It teaches that humans evolved from less sophisticated forms of animal life and so belief in the two first humans making conscious decision to rebel is senseless. Even reading the fall story symbolically does not get rid of the obsession of associating sin with sex in Christianity.

Exercise: Ian Barbour (Religion and Science, SCM, 2000) says that Augustine's insights into love and friendship can still be utilised, but less so his work on the Fall. Write an explanation in support of this and one challenge.

2. The challenge of psychology proposes sex to be an important and natural aspect of human development; whereas Augustine's thoughts only make sex necessary for reproduction. Freud argues sin is not a 'human disorder' transmitted by sex. For Freud, religion perpetuates guilt and sexual repression.

Exercise: Both Freud and Augustine can be seen to show how the misuse of sex and relationships leads to individual and social disorder. How?

3. Modern views of morality, such as Kant's, pose a more optimistic view of human nature – that reason, and not God's grace, is the source of salvation. There are no innate defects in human nature. We do behave selfishly sometimes but being moral tries to supersede animalistic inclinations. Correctly-educated reason can help overcome base instincts and help achieve peace.

4. Jean-Paul Sartre claims an essential human nature would mean we would not be free to develop our own personalities and by this, free will would be meaningless. To sin, for Sartre, would be to live according to a stereotype of what it is to be human and this would be to avoid living 'authentically'. Sartre called this 'mauvaise foi'. There is nothing to guarantee we are 'living right' and so authentic living can be filled with anxiety.

Exercise: Do you think we can align Sartre's thoughts on authentic living with belief in God?

Essay Skills

Types of Questions

Questions on this topic might focus on Augustine's teaching on human nature – including human relationships pre- and post-Fall, original sin and its effects on the will and human societies, and God's grace. Whichever it asks, candidates should always use the other in evaluation. Some examples of questions you might be asked are these:

Question: To what extent is Augustine's view of human nature pessimistic?

Here, assess extent to which humans can be saved according to Augustine – link to election, God's grace. Niebuhr's idea that it is pessimistic but necessary.

Question: "There is no distinctive human nature." Discuss.

In this essay, consider Augustine's portrayal of human nature as flawed and coherency of his reasons; compare with Sartre and Dawkins.

Question: "Augustine's teaching on a historical Fall and Original Sin is wrong." Discuss.

Assess the strengths of the challenges to Augustine from evolutionary biology, psychology and modern views on morality.

To what extent does Augustine's teaching on human nature mean that humans can never be morally good? Linked to pessimism essay – what does it mean to be 'morally good' – is this only enabled by God's grace or is it possible through our own reasoning (humanitarian principle)?

Exercise: Analyse this question: 'There is no distinctive human nature." Discuss.

Essay Skills – Introductions and Thesis Statement

Your introduction should:

1. indicate to the reader that you know what the question is about;

2. demonstrate the parameters of the question giving a sense of the two main sides of the argument; and

3. make clear where the essay will go, giving a clear thesis statement.

Exercise: Take this question: 'Augustine's views on human nature are absurd and dangerous." Discuss.

Write an introduction making all three parts of the introduction clear and distinct. One sentence is enough for each, but make sure each sentence is clear and concise.

1.   Definition and context: Identify what the question is about and relate this to Dawkins' position.

2. Parameters and opposition: State the opposing position, the position of Augustine.

3. Thesis statement: Make it clear where you stand, with Augustine, Dawkins or somewhere between. Be concise, outlining what your position is.

Death and the Afterlife

Structure of Thought

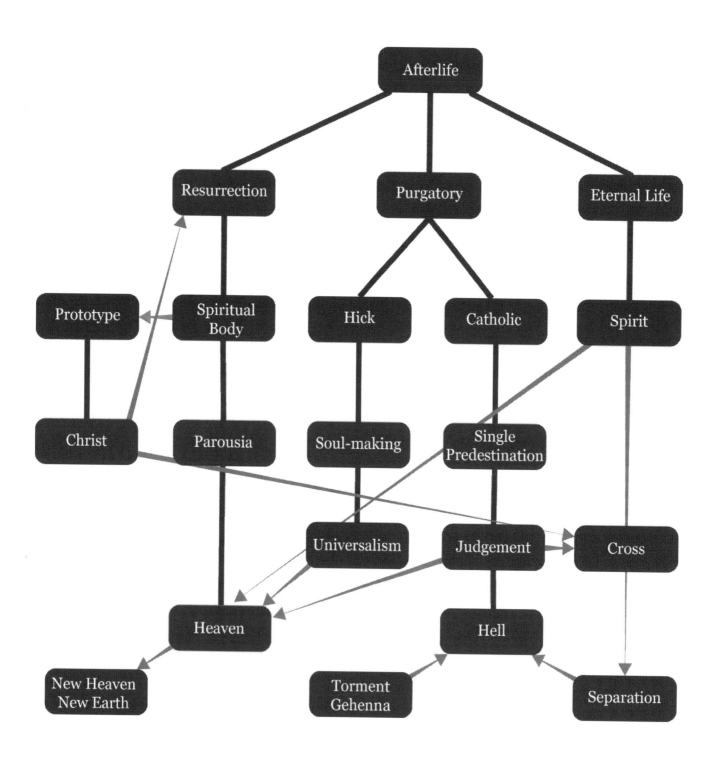

Christian teaching on Heaven, Hell, and Purgatory

Different Christian Teachings

Jesus' teaching on death and the afterlife is rooted in the Jewish tradition and eschatology of his time. Greek notions of the soul and immortality were also an influence. Jesus taught that his life and death were a sacrifice – an atonement for sin that would bring about a new kingdom.

Exercise: Define the key terms – Pharisees, Parousia, Kingdom of God, Hades, Gehenna,

Sheol, Sadducees, millenarianism, mortal sin, venial sin, perdition, apokatastasis

Different teachings include belief in heaven, hell and purgatory as actual places, as spiritual states, and as symbols of a person's spiritual and moral life on earth.

Exercise: Which of the three ideas above seems most coherent to you? Why?

The 'Kingdom' and its Problems

Jesus taught the 'Kingdom' to be three-fold:

1. A present moral and spiritual state calling for reform now – a call to reach out for the oppressed, seen in his parables.

2. A future redeemed state – made possible by Jesus' death and resurrection.

3. A place of punishment and justice – where the wicked suffer and those who suffered will prosper – seen in Jesus' beatitudes (Matthew 5). The issue here is: on what grounds are people divided between sheep (blessed) and goats (damned)? We examine this in the next section on Matthew 25.

Exercise: How far can we say that these three ideas about the Kingdom can be true together?

Exercise: Do you agree with Bultmann (extract on facing page) that literal resurrection is unbelievable to the modern mind?

"The resurrection of Jesus is just as difficult for modern man, if it means an event whereby a living supernatural power is released which can henceforth be appropriated through sacraments. To the biologist such language is meaningless, for he does not regard death as a problem at all. The idealist would not object to the idea of a life immune from death, but he could not believe that such a life is made inevitable by the resuscitation of a dead person. If that is the way God makes life available for man, his action is inextricably involved in a nature miracle. Such a notion he finds incomprehensible, for he can see God at work only in the reality of his personal life and in his transformation. But quite apart from the incredibility of such a miracle, he cannot see how an event like this could be the act of God, or how it could effect his own life. And as for the pre-existence of Christ, with its corollary of man's translation into a celestial realm of light, and the clothing of the human personality in heavenly robes and a spiritual body, all this is not only irrational but utterly meaningless. Why should salvation take this articular form?" (Rudolf Bultmann, 1941)

There is some confusion as to final judgement versus individual judgement. Furthermore, purgatory does not seem to be a Biblical idea – more, a teaching that arises out of human thought on the need for an opportunity to be forgiven, and an explanation of where people go between death and resurrection at the last day. There is ambiguity as to where this 'Kingdom' will be.

Hell

There are similarly different ideas about Hell. Origen described Hell as a spiritual state of someone separated from God; while Gregory of Nyssa described Hell as a guilty conscience before Christ. For Dante, Hell is the antithesis to Heaven; while for Tillich, Hell is a symbol of alienation:

"Heaven and hell must be taken seriously as metaphors for one of the two polar ultimates. in the experience of the divine" (Tillich, P, Systematic theology III, 1964, p. 446),

Lastly, for Catholics, Hell is an eternal separation from God for those who have committed mortal sins.

Hell serves two purposes. First, because thereby the Divine justice is safeguarded which is acceptable to God for its own sake. Secondly, the doctrine is useful, because the elect rejoice therein, when they see God's justice in them, and realise they have escaped them. For mortal sin which is contrary to charity a person is expelled for ever from the fellowship of the saints and condemned to everlasting punishment. (Aquinas, Summa Theologica)

Purgatory

Purgatory is often seen as a Catholic and Protestant way of providing the possibility of repentance outside of this mortal life. There is no clear teaching on this in the New Testament. For Catholics, purgatory represents a stage in the soul's journey to salvation with prayers for the dead dating back to pre-Christ. Some Protestants reject purgatory on the basis of lack of Biblical support. There is one clear mention of a possible purgatory, in Peter's first letter:

"Having been made alive, Jesus went and preached to the spirits in prison". (1 Peter 3:19)

Alternatively, Ambrose suggested that purgatory was a foretaste of Heaven and Hell; while Origen likened it to a probationary school.

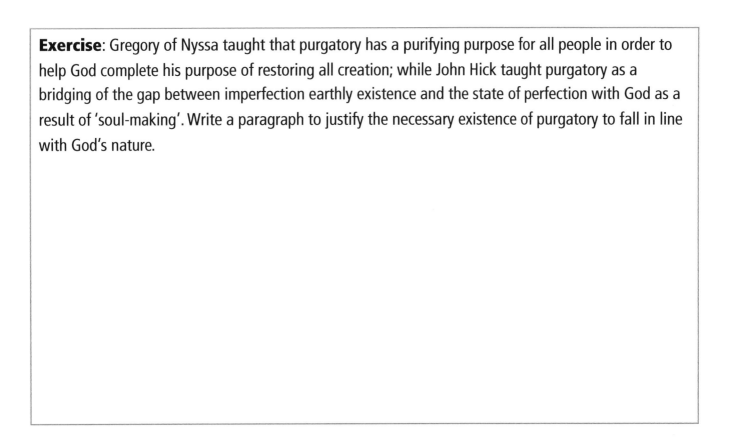

Exercise: Gregory of Nyssa taught that purgatory has a purifying purpose for all people in order to help God complete his purpose of restoring all creation; while John Hick taught purgatory as a bridging of the gap between imperfection earthly existence and the state of perfection with God as a result of 'soul-making'. Write a paragraph to justify the necessary existence of purgatory to fall in line with God's nature.

Election

There are different Christian ideas about who will be saved, including limited election (only a few will be saved); unlimited election (that all people are called to salvation but not all are saved); and universalist belief (that all people will be saved).

Exercise: Draw/choose an image to represent the three main ideas above.

Exercise: Which of the three ideas seems most in line with an omnibenevolent, omniscient and omnipotent God?

A further two ideas are limited atonement (sometimes called limited election) – the idea that Christ dies only for the sins of the Elect; and unlimited atonement (or election) – the idea that Christi died for the sins of the whole world.

Universalist belief

The idea that all people will be saved seems necessitate by a belief in an all-loving and all good God. It would seem wrong for a person's upbringing to exclude them from being reconciled with God and the fact we have free will implies that salvation should at least be possible for all.

John Hick – Jesus' resurrection triumphs over death. Jesus' God is not exclusivist.

Single and Double Predestination

Single predestination is the idea that God elects only those going to Heaven. Supported by Catholic teaching, Thomas Aquinas said that the Fall did not wipe out human free will. For Catholics, hell is the result of a wilful turning away from God – no one is predestined for Hell.

Exercise: Consider the quotation on the next page. In what sense can God elect for Heaven and not simultaneously be electing for Hell those he has not elected for Heaven? How coherent is the Catholic teaching?

"God predestines no one to go to Hell; for this, a wilful turning away from God (a mortal sin) is necessary, and persistence in it until the end" (Catechism of the Catholic Church para. 1037).

Interpreting Matthew 25 (Sheep & Goats)

Matthew 25 is a key text on Death and the Afterlife because it seems to suggest a basis upon which human beings are judged. First we must read the parable and place it in the context of the whole gospel of Matthew and the New Testament teaching on salvation.

Matthew 25: 31-The Parable of the Sheep and the Goats

"When he finally arrives, blazing in beauty and all his angels with him, the Son of Man will take his place on his glorious throne. Then all the nations will be arranged before him and he will sort the people out, much as a shepherd sorts out sheep and goats, putting sheep to his right and goats to his left.

"Then the King will say to those on his right, 'Enter, you who are blessed by my Father! Take what's coming to you in this kingdom. It's been ready for you since the world's foundation. And here's why:

I was hungry and you fed me,
I was thirsty and you gave me a drink,
I was homeless and you gave me a room,
I was shivering and you gave me clothes,
I was sick and you stopped to visit,
I was in prison and you came to me.'

"Then those 'sheep' are going to say, 'Master, what are you talking about? When did we ever see you hungry and feed you, thirsty and give you a drink? And when did we ever see you sick or in prison and come to you?' Then the King will say, 'I'm telling the solemn truth: Whenever you did one of these things to someone overlooked or ignored, that was me—you did it to me.'

"Then he will turn to the 'goats,' the ones on his left, and say, 'Get out, worthless goats! You're good for nothing but the fires of hell. And why? Because—

I was hungry and you gave me no meal,
I was thirsty and you gave me no drink,
I was homeless and you gave me no bed,
I was shivering and you gave me no clothes,
Sick and in prison, and you never visited.'

"Then those 'goats' are going to say, 'Master, what are you talking about? When did we ever see you hungry or thirsty or homeless or shivering or sick or in prison and didn't help?'

"He will answer them, 'I'm telling the solemn truth: Whenever you failed to do one of these things to someone who was being overlooked or ignored, that was me—you failed to do it to me.'

"Then those 'goats' will be herded to their eternal doom, but the 'sheep' to their eternal reward." (The Message, © 2002 by Eugene H. Peterson)

Exercise: How might we answer the question - on what basis are we judged, from Matthew 25?

Feminist/Liberationist Hermeneutic of Matthew 25

In the following passage from a research thesis on Feminism and Matthew's Gospel, the author shows how a liberationist perspective might be adopted.

All the nations gathered before the Son of Man are separated as a shepherd separates sheep from goats. While every individual has distinct biological and sociocultural characteristics, these differences do not provide the basis for their separation.

These differences between members of the nation cannot account for inferiority or criteria for judgment; rather, as revealed in the following verses, every individual is judged for what they have done for the least of these. Before the judge there is neither Jew nor Greek, slave nor free, male nor female, heterosexual nor homosexual, black nor white, rich nor poor (adapted from Galatians 3:28). Instead, those who looked out for those who are seen as different and inferior are placed on the right side.

In addressing those on the right, the Son of Man proclaims them blessed by the Father. We should not understand this language as a proclamation of God's gender, or an understanding of God as our literal Father, but as a metaphor for understanding our relationship to God. As human beings —and not omniscient divine beings—our language is necessarily insufficient when describing God. Not only is this idea present in Scripture but also in metaphysical theology. Since God is omnipotent, omnipresent, omniscient, and without beginning or end, it is impossible for our minds to fully comprehend God because we are finite beings.

Therefore, we can only attempt to understand the nature of God through metaphors—a process Sallie McFague calls metaphorical theology. Father, in this verse, must be understood as a metaphor for one aspect of our relationship to God. If we interpret this as a literal description of God's gender, we run the risk of our language becoming idolatrous. According to McFague, religious language is idolatrous when we forget our human insufficiencies and allow our anthropomorphised images to be taken literally. God is literally a Father; Scripture can only be read literally. In doing so, the human depictions we use to describe God affects "the way we feel about ourselves, for these images are 'divinised' and hence raised in status." One image of God is elevated above others, allowing some people to feel elevated above others because they are made more like this specific image of God.

An ecofeminist theology, as is Sallie McFague's metaphorical theology, helps us examine relational images of God and bring to light images that are often ignored. In doing so, we are able to better understand the relational aspect of God and how that influences our understanding of what it means to be made in the image of God. We should, therefore, understand this blessing from our Father God as a blessing from our Mother God, lover God, friend God, saviour God, and so on.

The six acts of service should be recognised not only on the level of individuals helping other individuals, but also on the level of collective individuals wrestling with structural injustices. When considering those who are hungry, what are we doing to respond to a nation that over-consumes food while one in nine people worldwide suffer from chronic undernourishment? When giving drink to the poor, how do we respond as a nation to the water crisis in Flint, Michigan? Beyond what we do for the individual strangers in our life, what are we doing to take care of immigrants and refugees? When an order proposes that we ban immigrants from Iran, Libya, Somalia, Sudan, Syria, and Yemen, how do we respond? (The Way Forward Matthew 25:31-46 – The Least of These Then and Now, Katarina von Kühn, unpublished thesis)

Exercise: How does Katarina von Kuhn interpret 'the least of these'? Who are they?

31

Thinking Through Matthew 25

We need to try to understand two different perspectives on Matthew 25 - amongst others. Let's call them the liberationist and literalist (conservative evangelical) interpretations.

Theme	Liberationist	Conservative Evangelical
Sheep	Those pursuing justice and attempting to alleviate social sin by their practical actions.	Those members of God's kingdom trying to help out those brothers and sisters - fellow Christians - less well off than themselves.
Goats	Those ignoring issues of social justice caused by structural sin, and doing nothing.	Those failing to respond to anyone in the church (ie Christians) who have fallen on hard times or need other forms of support.
Heaven	A state of reality realised by building systems of justice	A place that exists after death and judgement on the basis of compassion for God's people in need.
Hell	A state of reality in which people suffer the consequences of structural sin by being separated and alienated from each other.	A place after judgement where those who have failed to love their brothers and sisters in need are consigned to everlasting torment.

Calvin, Predestination and Matthew 25

God foreknows what will happen but His will is hidden from the limited knowledge of humans. Even if God has chosen particular individuals, both the elect and the non-elect have a duty to act morally and the Christian duty is to spread God's word to all kinds of people. Calvin's interpretation of the parable fo the Sheep and the Goats shows how the doctrinal and cultural lenses through which we view Scripture affects the interpretation.

1. Calvin's commentary on verse 34, for example, illustrates how nothing can be allowed to distract us from the key Reformation doctrine of justification by faith: "But before speaking of the reward of good works, he points out, in passing, that the commencement of salvation flows from a higher source; for by calling them blessed of the Father, he reminds them, that their salvation proceeded from the undeserved favour of God'. We are saved, Calvin reasserts, by the 'underserved favour of God' (doctrine of grace).

2. Verse 41 of Matthew 25 speaks of everlasting fire of damnation, and Calvin takes a metaphorical view of this description (in other words, to Calvin hell is not a literal place of torment by fire).

"He casts the damned into everlasting fire. We have stated formerly, that the term fire represents metaphorically that dreadful punishment which our senses are unable to comprehend. It is therefore unnecessary to enter into subtle inquiries, as the sophists do, into the materials or form of this fire; for there would be equally good reason to inquire about the worm, which Isaiah connects with the fire for their worm shall not die, neither shall their fire be quenched, (Isaiah 66:24).

Besides, the same prophet shows plainly enough in another passage that the expression is metaphorical; for he compares the Spirit of God to a blast by which the fire is kindled, and adds a mixture of brimstone, Under these words, therefore, we ought to represent to our minds the future vengeance of God against the wicked, which, being more grievous than all earthly torments, ought rather to excite horror than a desire to know it. But we must observe the eternity of this fire, as well as of the glory which, a little before, was promised to believers." (Calvin's Commentary on Matthew 25:41)

Exercise: Find quotations from Matthew 25, or examples, to support the following claims:

1. We should pursue justice for the marginalised, without thinking of the heavenly reward (religious observance is not enough).

2. The reward is for ALL who pursue justice, not just Christians (an interpretation against Calvin's view above, or the conservative evangelical view considered in the table above).

---

3. Jesus' list of acts that would be rewarded is supported in his own ministry of healing and social teaching.

4. We are obliged to help all in need, not just those in our own social group, or from our church.

Thought Point (Hick)

In the Pluralism section of the Christian Thought paper, Hick argues for Universal Pluralism – that all religions contain part of the Divine Reality (Inclusivism). Notice how the name of Christ retreats into the background in Hick's thought. In Protestant Christianity there is a divide between those who argue for Free Will (like John Wesley, founder of Methodism) and those from the Calvinist tradition (such as the Church of Scotland) arguing for double predestination of both the saved and the damned. Most recoil against the idea that babies are damned for eternity from birth, unless we invoke some special idea of God as the timeless one as Boethius does. The Catholic church has a doctrine of single predestination - predestination of the saved.

To God, all moments of time are present in their immediacy. When therefore he establishes his eternal plan of 'predestination,' he includes in it each person's free response to his grace: "In this city, in fact, both Herod and Pontius Pilate, with the Gentiles and the peoples of Israel, gathered together against your holy servant Jesus, whom you anointed, to do whatever your hand and your plan had predestined to take place" [Acts 4:27-28]. For the sake of accomplishing his plan of salvation, God permitted the acts that flowed from their blindness. (Catechism)

Thought Point (Boethius)

In Philosophy of Religion Boethius argues God foreknows because he is outside time. To foreknow doesn't necessarily mean God predestines. The Catholic Catechism (above) seems to say something similar about God and time.

Essay Skills

Types of Questions

Questions on this topic might focus on Christian teaching on heaven, hell or purgatory, or on election. Whichever it asks, candidates should always use the other in evaluation. Some examples of questions you might be asked are these:

Q. Critically assess the claim that God's judgement takes place immediately after death.

A. This asks you to compare the coherency of claims of immediate vs final judgement. Make use of the parable of Lazarus and the rich man and arguments concerning purgatory.

Q. Assess the view that purgatory is a state through which everyone goes.

A. Critically compare the Catholic belief that it is, and Hick's views of purification of the soul to be in God's presence, with ideas of immediate judgement made possible by Christ's sacrifice.

Q. To what extent are heaven and hell eternal?

A. Assess Aquinas' idea of heaven being timeless Beatific Vision, Augustine's arguments of eternal Heaven and Hell; vs ideas of permanency of hell conflicting with belief in a just God.

Q. "Heaven is the transformation and perfection of the whole of creation." Discuss.

A. Critically compare ideas in Revelations 21:1, concept of Parousia; with Barth's ideas that Heaven is not a single event but in the resurrection and Pentecost etc. Also assess the ideas that this transformation is in the hands of Christians today.

Essay Skills – Introductions and Thesis Statement

Your introduction should:

1. indicate to the reader that you know what the question is about;

2. demonstrate the parameters of the question giving a sense of the two main sides of the argument; and

3. make clear where the essay will go, giving a clear thesis statement.

Exercise: Take this question: 'Purgatory is a state through which everyone goes.' Discuss.

Write an introduction making all three parts of the introduction clear and distinct. One sentence is enough for each, but make sure each sentence is clear and concise.

1. Definition and context: Identify what the question is about and the Catholic position.

2. Parameters and opposition: State the opposing position, the position of some Protestant thinkers (such as the Reformers Calvin and Luther)..

---

3. Thesis statement: Make it clear where you stand, with Catholicism, Protestantism or somewhere between. Be concise, outlining what your position is.

Knowledge of God's Existence

Structure of Thought

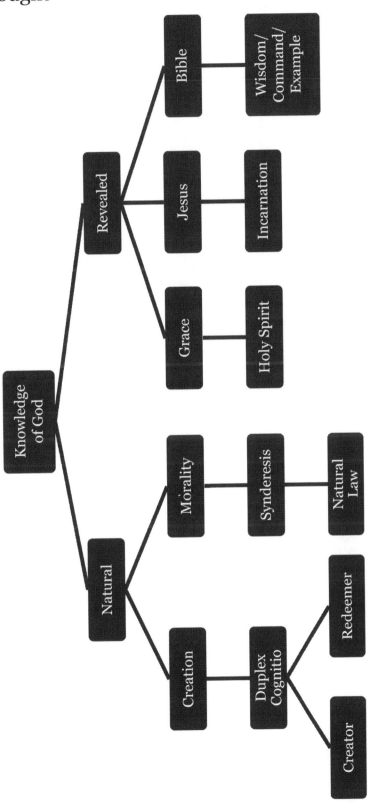

Natural Knowledge of God's Existence – Innate Human Sense

The idea that we have an innate sense of the divine comes, in part, from the belief that we are made in imago dei. Being made in God's image gives us an inbuilt capacity and desire to know God.

This inbuilt capacity and desire is reflected in human openness to beauty and goodness as aspects of God; as well as our human intellectual ability to reflect on and recognise God's existence.

Exercise: Give a brief explanation of the main difference between natural theology and revealed theology. Do you think one is more reliable than the other?

Belief in knowledge of God as innate is supported by Calvin ('sensus divinitatis') and the Catechism of the Catholic Church.

Exercise: To what extent do you agree with Calvin's idea of 'semen religionis' (seed of religion) – the idea that humans have an inclination to carry out religious practices? Give evidence for and against and make a judgement.

Thought Point (Connections)

In Aquinas' Natural Law theory of morality, synderesis means we possess the 'intuitive knowledge of first principles' – the primary precepts orientate us towards the good to build the flourishing life (Eudaimonia).

The Catechism of the Catholic Church said "one may well call man a religious being." This is supported by Cicero and Calvin's ideas of 'universal consent' – that God must exist, since so many people believe in a God/gods. Scriptural evidence for this is Acts 17:16-34.

Exercise: Look up this passage in Acts. How could it be used to support the idea of mankind being 'religious'?

Human Openness to Beauty and Goodness as Aspects of God

Natural Law teaches that we have an innate awareness of justice, while Catholic and Calvinist ideas of conscience suggest a 'joint knowledge' between humans and God, giving them an internal moral awareness. Veritatis Splendor (1995 encyclical) speaks of

'contemplation of beauty' as an interpretation of the primary precept 'Worship of God'.

Human Intellectual Ability to Reflect on and Recognise God's Existence

This idea is recognised in Thomas Aquinas' Five Ways. Here, God is understood as the Uncaused Cause of all, sustaining all. As a necessary existence, God is understood to exist differently to other beings.

Natural Knowledge of God's Existence – as seen in the Order of Creation

The idea that the appearance of design and purpose in nature leads to knowledge of God –

seen notably in Paley's teleological argument for the existence of God. The apparent order in nature lends itself to revelation of God as Creator.

Exercise: Can you list natural examples of apparent order and purpose?

Calvin proposed that human minds are finite – limited. This means that reason is not enough to stand alone in revealing God – He must also make Himself known through creation.

Exercise: Consider Calvin's quote below. Imagine Calvin has been asked 'what do you mean by this?' Write a reply.

What we know of God through creation is "a sort of mirror in which we can contemplate God, who is otherwise invisible." (John Calvin: Institutes I.V1).

William Paley's argument from design concluded the existence of an infinitely powerful designer of the natural world – God. However, this has been challenged by Hume and Dawkins – both of whom suggest that nature seems more cruel than beautiful.

Exercise: What is the response of process theology to challenges to Paley's argument?

Another idea about God that differs to classical theology, is the idea that God participates in nature and suffers with creation, being revealed in every moment of creation. Process theology is this idea of God working 'with' the natural processes.

Exercise: To what extent does the idea of God suffering with creation add consolation to those who use the existence of evil and suffering to argue against the existence of God?

New Natural Theology of Alister McGrath

Alister McGrath is Professor of Theology at Oxford and heads up a movement to rehabilitate natural theology. He argues that natural theology took a wrong turning attempting to prove the existence of God using, for example, Paley's argument from Design. Effectively the natural theologian took the tools of the Enlightenment and its methods of proof and verification - but neither are appropriate to the task, and also, the role of natural theology under Augustine was different. It was to provide a **fiduciary framework**, or framework of faith which makes sense of all reality, both scientific (the origin of the Universe) and metaphysical, (the place of truth, beauty and love in human experience). Of course, God is part of the metaphysical structure and the issue is, does belief in God produce a better fit of the evidence before us, both measurable and metaphysical? Here's a sample of his writing:

Natural theology is about seeing nature in such a way that it points beyond itself to a transcendent reality, without itself constituting that reality. Nature is not itself supernatural; yet the supernatural is disclosed in and through the natural. The relevance of the point about the call of Samuel to any Christian engagement with nature will therefore be clear. We are invited, as ones who are part of the natural order and who stand within that realm of nature, to see nature as pointing beyond itself to the realm of the transcendent. Moments of epiphany do not require us to stand outside the realm of nature, nor need they be mediated through what might be called "supernatural" means. Christian theology has long recognized that the divine may be disclosed through the mundane; that God may be known through things of this world.

It is therefore important to lay down a fundamental challenge to any approach to natural theology which assumes that God is absent from the natural world, and fails to speak through its genres. Revelation is not supernatural, as this unhelpful term is traditionally understood. As the story of Samuel and countless other biblical narratives make clear, divine revelation does not take place in the heavens, but here on earth, in the midst of the commonplaces of life. Perhaps Charles Williams' idea of "arch-nature" deserves more careful consideration than it has traditionally received. God is present in this world, and makes himself known in the world of human experience, inspiring a sense of awe, mystery, and wonder. The whole point of the Christian doctrine of revelation is that God elicits such a response from humanity through self-revelation adapted or "accommodated" (Calvin) to the familiar realities of this world, in order to form a bridge between earth and heaven, nature and grace. This perceptible acceleration of interest in natural theology was partly – though not totally – due to a perception within the English Christian church that an appeal to the regularity of nature would be much more effective and productive in the public arena than reliance on a sacred text which was increasingly regarded with suspicion. Natural theology was thus seen as an especially promising apologetic tool in a cultural situation which had witnessed significant erosion in the esteem in which Christianity's sacred texts were held. If an appeal to the Bible no longer carried weight, might an appeal to that more public text of nature itself prove decisive? It was ultimately a forlorn hope. But that crushing sense of disappointment, as it turned out, took some considerable time to crystallise.

If one can speak of a "golden age of natural theology" this may reasonably be argued to occupy a period of a century and a half, beginning in the late seventeenth century, and ending in the first half of the nineteenth. It is not difficult to understand why. The rise of the Newtonian worldview gave natural theology a new lease of life, as the celebrated "Boyle Lectures" make clear.

This approach seemed to lead to Deism, rather than to orthodox Christianity. God tends to be presented and understood as the extension of accepted human ideas of justice, rationality, and wisdom. This apologetic approach does not necessarily lead away from Christianity; nevertheless, it is certainly not well disposed towards Christian specifics.

Alarmingly, some of the most influential Boyle lecturers were Arians, committed to a thoroughly rationalist understanding of Christ.

Richard Dawkins speaks for many when he argues that a Darwinian world has no goal or purpose, and we delude ourselves if we think otherwise. The universe is neither good nor evil, and cannot be *considered to be moving towards any specific goal.*

·In a universe of blind physical forces and genetic replication, some people are going to get hurt, other people are going to get lucky, and you won't find any rhyme or reason in it, nor any justice. The universe we observe had precisely the properties we should expect if there is, at bottom, no design, no purpose, no evil and no good, nothing but blind pitiless indifference." (Richard Dawkins, River out of Eden: A Darwinian View of Life. London: Phoenix, page 133). Extract from A.E. McGrath , The Order of Things, Explorations in Scientific Theology page 78-80)

Exercise: Why might natural theology, wrongly handled, lead to Deism?

Revealed Knowledge of God's Existence – Faith & Grace

Another argument is that our finite minds make it so that natural knowledge is not sufficient as a source of knowledge of God. Faith and grace are also needed. Calvin's view was **si**

Integer stetisset Adam. This is the idea that if Adam had not sinned, everyone could be in the knowledge of God. The Catholic Church teaches that the Fall generated a confusion in human desire for God but it did not separate humans from God completely.

Catholic teaching does not separate faith from reason. They argue that faith needs reason in order for it to have meaning.

Exercise: Explain the difference between Aquinas' formed and unformed faith.

Calvin described faith as being firm and certain knowledge revealed through Christ and the Holy Spirit; as well as a willingness to believe that is assured spiritually and emotionally. A person's relationship with God is completed by God's grace – faith alone is not enough.

For Aquinas, faith can only be justified by grace through the Holy Spirit; while for Calvin, the damage caused by Original Sin is healed by the gift of the Holy Spirit.

Exercise: Consider the quotes below. What do they suggest about human knowledge of God? How could you critique them?

1. "For what can be known about God is plain to them, because God has shown it to them" (St Paul: Letter to the Romans 1:19-20).

---

2. *"In this ruin of mankind no one now experiences God…until Christ the Mediator comes forward to reconcile him to us". (John Calvin: Institutes I.II.1).*

Revealed Knowledge of God's Existence – in Jesus Christ

The suggestion that the Bible should be read from a Trinitarian perspective includes God as Father – through the prophets; as Christ the mediator – giving clarity to God's promises; and as Holy Spirit – through inspired Christians.

Catholic teaching agrees with Calvinist views of Christ as a mediator and mirror of God, but says that the significance of revelation should continue with our faith.

While Christianity cannot be 'reduced' to the Bible (as the doctrinal statements emerged hundreds of years later at church councils), the Bible nevertheless remains a significant source for knowledge of God – a knowledge that is personal and collective.

Exercise: Consider the quote below. How might it support both the importance of the Bible and the Church as a source of knowledge of God?

"God is the author of sacred Scripture...[and its words are] the speech of God as it is put down in writing under the breath of the Holy Spirit" (Catechism, para. 105).

Exercise: Read the arguments below and assess whether they support or disagree with the idea that natural knowledge is the same as revealed knowledge of God.

1. Things exist because God has chosen them to and in this way, God remains the source of all knowledge and has revealed everything that it is possible for us to know anything about.

2. Natural knowledge is reached through reason, while revealed knowledge is reached through faith.

3. God can reveal things to us through our reason (Aquinas) and this allows us to learn more about God.

4. Types of knowledge revealed through reason or faith are different. E.g. Trinity and life after death = revealed and not available through natural revelation.

Exercise: Look up and read Romans 1:18-21. What relevance does this have to natural or revealed knowledge of God? Explain.

Thought Point (Connections)

Although Jesus claims to 'fulfil the law' (possible translation 'accomplish its purpose'), nonetheless he overturns much of the Levitical purity code (see Leviticus 18, part of the Torah or Law). He works on the Sabbath, picking corn, redefines purity not in terms of food, but internal moral sin (Mark 7), and allows an unclean woman (unclean because she's bleeding) to touch him (Mark 5). Joseph Fletcher would see Jesus' ethics as situational because Jesus elevates agape love above everything (as in the Parable of the Good Samaritan in Luke).

Essay Skills

Types of questions

Questions on this topic might focus on innate natural knowledge of God, knowledge of God through apparent design, grace and faith as revealed knowledge of God, and God as revealed through the person of Jesus Christ. Whichever it asks, candidates should always use aspects of the other topics in evaluation. Some examples of questions you might be asked are these:

Q. To what extent can God not be known through reason alone?

A. Consider the strengths of natural theology as a sound and rational basis for faith; vs the strength of Barth's claim that it would be arrogant to think fallible human reason could lead to full knowledge of God.

Q. "The Fall has completely removed all natural human knowledge of God." Discuss.

A. Consider Augustine's view of the Fall corrupting human will and therefore knowledge of God; vs Aquinas' view of our God given reason allowing the aid of both natural and revealed theology.

Q. To what extent is faith sufficient reason for belief in God's existence?

A. Consider the strength of sensus divinitatis vs criticisms that theistic knowledge is irrational.

Q. Critically assess the claim that natural knowledge of God is the same as revealed knowledge of God.

A. Consider strength of claim that God is source of all knowledge, even through our reason; and the importance of the difference between natural knowledge reached through reason and revealed knowledge reached through faith.

Exercise: Analyse this question: 'To what extent has the Fall completely removed all natural human knowledge of God?

Essay Skills – Introductions and Thesis Statement

Your introduction should:

1. indicate to the reader that you know what the question is about;

2. demonstrate the parameters of the question giving a sense of the two main sides of the argument; and

3. make clear where the essay will go, giving a clear thesis statement.

Exercise: Take this question: 'God cannot be known through reason alone.' Discuss.

Write an introduction making all three parts of the introduction clear and distinct. One sentence is enough for each, but make sure each sentence is clear and concise.

1. Definition and context: Identify what the question is about and the position of natural theology.

---

2. Parameters and opposition: State the opposing position e.g. Douglas Hedley's views that reason needs to be accompanied by imagination when discussing philosophy; or Barth's view that human knowledge is fallible and so cannot, alone, reach God.

3. Thesis statement: Make it clear where you stand, with the use of reason, the role of faith or somewhere between. Be concise, outlining what your position is.

The Person of Jesus Christ

Structure of Thought

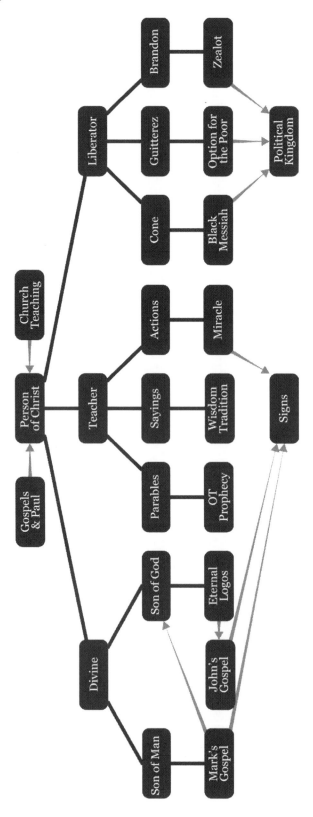

The Person of Jesus Christ

Jesus's authority is seen in his teachings and in the example he has set, as well as in his relationship with God. The different aspects of Jesus' authority, and questions of where this has come from, has allowed Jesus to be considered an authority even by non-Christians.

Two divergent ways of looking at the person of Jesus is the Jesus of history, and the Christ of faith. E.P. Sanders claimed that faith claims are different to those made in the realm of reason. Jesus did act within history and his teachings on hope for the outcasts did make him different to his contemporaries but not unique. By entering the realms of theology, we might confuse history with faith.

Conversely, Rudolf Bultmann argued that the Christ of faith was more important than the Jesus of history. Bultmann says we can know 'almost nothing' of the historical Jesus and instead, we should demythologise the Bible .

A final way of identifying Jesus is as 'black Messiah. James Cone identifies the origins of this title for Jesus as historical- in line with the suffering and oppression of black people. The wooden cross resonates, he says, with the 'lynching tree'. Jesus' suffering was in unity with the oppressed.

Exercise: Which of the identities, above, do you think is the most helpful way of understanding Jesus? Do you think it is helpful to consider Jesus from so many perspectives?

Jesus Christ's Authority as the Son of God

In this role, Jesus is seen to have come to bring salvation and to carry out God's will on Earth. This identity is evidence in Jesus' apparent knowledge of God, his miracles and his resurrection.

Two ways of approaching a study of Christ in the Biblical text are 'Christology from above' and 'Christology from below'. The first focuses on Jesus' divinity ('from above') and is known as high Christology. This reading relies on faith and cannot be proven. The second, 'Christology from below', focuses on Jesus' example and message and people's response to this. This is known as 'low Christology'. A low Christology approach might even view Jesus' miracles as parables.

Exercise: Do you think Jesus thought/ knew he was the Son of God? Use Exodus 3:14, John 14:6 and John 14:28 to help inform your answer.

Exercise: Remind yourself of (or research now) the heretical views of Nestorius, Apollinarius and the Docetic Christians. Which of these views, if any, do you think is most coherent and why?

Both high and low Christologies view some miracles as signs of salvation. For example, the healing of the man born blind in John 9:1-41 is more focused more on his awareness of Jesus as saviour, than on the actual process of his sight being restored. Another example is Jesus' walking on water in Mark 6:47-52 which seems to mirror God's hovering over the chaotic waters in the moment of creation of the world – implying salvation being extended to all.

Jesus' resurrection differed to that taught by the Pharisees. The Pharisees taught the raising of the righteous before God; whereas Jesus' resurrection was to be experienced by many over a long period, marking the start of a new era and a change of humankind's relationship with God. Wolfhart Pannenberg described Jesus' resurrection as the decisive moment in history.

Exercise: Read the case of 'doubting Thomas' in John 20:27-28. In what sense can the resurrection be seen to give authority to proclaim Jesus as the son of God?

Jesus Christ's Authority as a Teacher of Wisdom

In this role, Jesus is seen to develop Jewish ethics. Jesus' teachings include those on repentance and forgiveness, inner purity and moral motivation contained in the Torah (the first five books of the Bible).

Exercise: Look up Matthew 5:17-48 and Luke 15:11-32. Identify Jesus' teachings, their implications, and what they imply about Jesus' identity. Compare with Leviticus 18 (part of the Torah).

Wittgenstein said that Jesus affirmed living authentically, embodying both the spiritual and the moral. Jesus expresses his moral message through actions, parables and short sayings.

Exercise: Jesus is sometimes seen as the 'new Moses' establishing a New Israel, for example in the writings of N.T. Wright, former Bishop of Durham. How might Matthew 5:17 support this idea?

Jesus' teachings on forgiveness are at the heart of his teachings on the arrival of the Kingdom of God. Examples include the story of Zacchaeus and Jesus' Parable of the Lost Son. The importance of forgiveness is also seen in Jesus' teaching of the Lord's Prayer.

Jesus' teachings on social responsibility were evident in his teachings on the Sabbath which was an important religious law that he felt was being misused. The Sabbath entitled everyone to one day free from work a week. However, some used this as an excuse to avoid social responsibility. Indeed, 39 different definitions and examples of work to be avoided had been constructed, which led to focus on the religious duty rather than duty to humanity. Jesus demonstrated the need to be responsible for your fellow human by setting the example himself – he broke the Sabbath rules and allowed his disciples to pick corn on the Sabbath. Overall, Jesus' message was that religious practices should serve human needs.

Exercise: Find and write down the quote that supports this teaching in Mark 2:27.

Exercise: Do you agree that morality should not just be 'blind obedience'? Are there any moral laws to which we should be obedient?

Jesus Christ's Authority as a Liberator

In this role, Jesus is seen to challenge political and religious authorities. Jesus as liberator includes of the marginalised and of the poor. This is evident in Jesus' challenge both to political and religious authority.

S.G.F. Brandon argues in Jesus and the Zealots that Jesus was politically-driven and more of a freedom-fighter than the pacifist that later writers like to make him out to be. Jesus shows a bias to the 'preferential option for the poor' and 'the underside of history'.

Exercise: Define 'preferential option for the poor' and 'the underside of history'. Find scriptural evidence that supports Jesus' bias towards these two groups.

Exercise: Look up Mark 5:24-34 and Luke 10:25-37. What can these passages tell you about Jesus' role as a liberator? Is this the only side to Jesus shown in the passages or are allusions also made to his role as Son of God and teacher of wisdom?

Gustavo Gutiérrez Merino considered that seeing Jesus as 'liberator' made him 'really engaged' in the world, allowing us to move away from the Bible as being full of fiction characters. Jesus' mission was not so much national Zealot, as saviour of all human societies – not just Israel. He showed 'preferential option for the poor', setting the example for others to follow.

Camillo Torres Restrepo is an example of a Catholic Priest who left the priesthood to take up arms in active resistance against the government.

Exercise: Do you think violence can be justified within Christian moral teaching?

Many parables detail the help of outcasts. These include the sexually impure, tax collectors, diseased and the uneducated.

Exercise: What is the meaning of the Greek word 'hamartoloi'?

Exercise: Look up two miracles that show Jesus helping outcasts. Choose an image to represent each of these. (You might start at Mark chapter 2, or chapter 5).

Essay Skills

Types of questions

Questions on this topic might focus on Jesus Christ's authority as the Son of God, as teacher of wisdom or liberator. Whichever it asks, candidates should always use aspects of the others in evaluation. Some examples of questions you might be asked are these:

Q. "Jesus was no more than a teacher of wisdom." Discuss.

A. Consider in your answer, the views of Bultmann and Hick that we need to demythologise the Bible, leaving us with an authentic teacher of wisdom. Add in critique considering if anything would then Jesus apart from other teachers of wisdom and the view that the resurrection is a defining moment.

Q. To what extent was Jesus more than a liberator?

A. Compare ideas of his spiritual leadership with his political leadership.

Q. "Jesus thought he was divine." Discuss.

A. Compare evidence where Jesus talks about sin and death with authority with evidence of his humanity in Gethsemane and doctrines of Jesus being 'fully human'.

Q. To what extent would it be fair to say Jesus' relationship with God was 'very special' rather than 'truly unique'?

A. Consider Sanders' view that uniqueness cannot be verified historically and Macquarrie's suggestion that the question of uniqueness should be left alone. Compare with ideas about poignancy of Jesus' resurrection – the Christ-Event.

Exercise: Analyse this question: To what extent was Jesus only a teacher of wisdom?

Essay Skills – Introduction and Thesis Statement

Your introduction should:

1. indicate to the reader that you know what the question is about;

2. demonstrate the parameters of the question giving a sense of the two main sides of the argument;

3. make clear where the essay will go, giving a clear thesis statement.

Exercise: Take this question: 'Jesus was no more than a political liberator.' Discuss.

Write an introduction making all three parts of the introduction clear and distinct. One sentence is enough for each, but make sure each sentence is clear and concise.

1. Definition and context: Identify what the question is about and the perspective, perhaps, of a libertarian theologian.

2. Parameters and opposition: State the opposing position, the position of some who might say most importantly, Jesus was God's Son.

3. Thesis statement: Make it clear where you stand, with liberator, God's Son or somewhere between. Be concise, outlining what your position is.

Christian Moral Principles

Structure of Thought

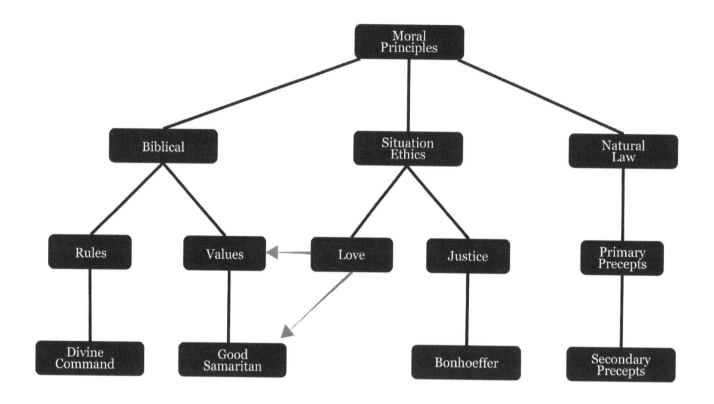

Christian Moral Principles in the Bible

The Bible as the only authority for Christian ethical practices

Exercise: What do you think 2 Timothy 3:16 means when it says the Bible is 'inspired' or "God-breathed'?

Exercise: Does it necessarily follow that if the Bible reveals God's will, then only Biblical ethical commands should be followed?

Theonomous (God-centred) ethics are shown through an example played out in the Bible e.g. King David's adultery with Bathsheba. This example shows what living the moral life 'is not'. Such ethics must be understood in the theological context of the life lived as a covenant with God.

Exercise: Ethics are both social and personal in the Old Testament. How is this shown in the 10 Commandments?

Karl Barth taught that a fully literalistic reading of the Bible could count as 'bibliolatry' – a false worship of the Bible. The words of the Bible can be seen as a 'witness' to God's Word (logo) revealed through the different writers of the Bible and so human reason must be taken into account, reading the Bible critically as a source of inspiration.

Exercise: Find examples in the Bible of teachings that if taken literally, could be dangerous/ unacceptable today. Do you think Barth's suggestion conflicts with any notion of the Bible as propositional revelation?

The New Testament is often seen as a renewal of Old Testament Law – for example, Matthew 5:38-42 shows reconciliation replacing retribution.

Exercise: Consider the statements below and identify each as a strength or as a weakness of the Bible as the only source of authority. Stretch yourself by giving a response to critique each strength or weakness and then a make a judgement as to overall, is it strong or weak.

1. Seeing the Bible as infallible can provide a helpful framework for living – decisions about taking life (Sermon on Mount); attitudes towards sexuality (Old Testament, St Paul); attitudes towards marriage (Genesis and Jesus' teachings).

2. The inspiration of the Holy Spirit (2 Timothy 3:16) makes the Bible infallible and inerrant.

3. We can't separate ourselves from our own reading of the text – impossible not to read subjectively and with interpretation.

4. Many Christians do not follow all the 'rules' in the Bible and some do not even appear to refer to the Old testament Code of living e.g. Leviticus 19:27 – limits the cutting of facial and head hair; Leviticus 19:19 bans planting two crops in the same field.

5. Richard Mouw – "just because there is one biblical commandment, a law of love, does not rule out the possibility of other biblical commandments on other matters" (Summarised and cited in Ahluwalia & Bowie, 2016, p. 392).

6. If God dictated, then why so many different styles e.g. John's Gospel is much more mystical and theological.

7. Can be trusted and relied upon.

8. Conflicts arise – Jesus' attitude to Jewish laws.

Thought Point (Connections)

In Religious Pluralism we find a spectrum of claims about biblical truth. The inerrantists are strong in America – see the Chicago Statement on Biblical Inerrancy (1978), signed by many academics such as the ethics writer Harry Gensler. Inerrantists tend to be exclusivists. They exclude other religions from any hope of salvation. John Hick sees bible truth as myth (a certain form of language containing some truth but requiring careful interpretation). Bultmann argues the same in the Philosophy of Religion Religious Language section.

Bible, Church, and Reason

Another view is that Christian ethics should combine biblical and Church teachings with human reason to account for new situations.

Exercise: What is the meaning of 'prima scriptura' and do you agree with this approach?

Richard Hays and William Spohn were of the opinion that scripture cannot be studied without reference to the church communities and traditions within which it operates.

Ethical Heteronomy (Law made by Others)

The Natural Law of Catholicism is made up of a Christian ethics that can be accessed through the natural world, Church authority, reason and conscience. It is universal because we all share the one rational human nature, and have God-given insight into morality by synderesis (the sense implanted in us of right and wrong)

Exercise: How might the idea of synderesis be supported by Romans 2:15?

Thomas Aquinas would support human experience of God's eternal law through our inclination to do good and avoid evil. He called this synderesis.

The Magisterium represent the collective wisdom of church leaders and teachers in Catholicism. Its views are published in Papal encyclical and is authoritative. The centrality of reason, conscience, Magisterium and natural law are reasserted in the 1996 encyclical Veritatis Splendor.

Exercise: Liberation theology was suspicious of 'top-down' traditional Church teaching. Do you think they were justified in this suspicion? Why?

Protestant views on Bible, Church and Reason

The Protestant similar to Catholicism but without Magisterium. Richard Hooker and Hugo Grotius taught that the bible evolved over time, developing out of the communities and so reason and conscience should be a guide to its use in ethics. Stanley Hauerwas claimed that Christian ethics can only be done in the Christian worshipping community and by practising Christian social virtues, Christians need to question society's values. Church tradition may change with time, but moral authority ultimately rests with the Bible.

Exercise: Draw a Venn diagram to identify similarities and differences between Catholic and Protestant approaches to Bible, Church and reason.

Autonomous Morality

Love (agape) as the only Christian ethical principle which governs Christian practices.

Love should be the only governing Christian principle – evident in Jesus' own sacrifice. Pope Francis encourages moral guidance rooted in love. We must recognise the modern challenges of human relationships while also recognising the rules of Catholic tradition.

Exercise: Jesus specifically challenged rule-based ethics. How is this evident in Mark 7:14-23?

Exercise: Think of two arguments in favour, and two arguments against, the claim that 'the principle of love is sufficient' in moral decision-making. You could make links to situation ethics (for yes) and the Sermon on the Mount, Matthew 5, (for no).

Essay Skills

Types of questions

Questions on this topic might focus on Christian teaching on the Bible as the only authority, the role of Bible, Church and reason, or love as the only Christian ethical principle.

Whichever it asks, candidates should always use the other in evaluation. Some examples of questions you might be asked are these:

Q. To what extent are Christian ethics distinctive?

A. Essentially, this considers the extent to which Christian ethics are deontological or relative. Are they set apart from ethics that use reason? Do they differ to the values of society? To what extent?

Q. "Christian ethics are more communal than personal." Discuss.

A. How far are the ethics and teachings of Jesus focused on the individual, compared with the individual as part of a collective people of God.

Q. To what extent is the principle of love sufficient to live a good life?

A. Consider situation ethics and appeal to secular western culture, vs everything in addition to love that is also taught e.g. in Sermon on the Mount.

Q. Assess the view that the Bible is a comprehensive moral guide.

A. To what extent can the Bible provide a voice for all situations? Or, is it rooted in a particular cultural community, reflecting limitations of their time? Think of the many moral issues not specifically mentioned in the Bible (contraception, abortion, principles of just war for example).

Exercise: Analyse this question: 'The Church should decide what is morally good." Discuss.

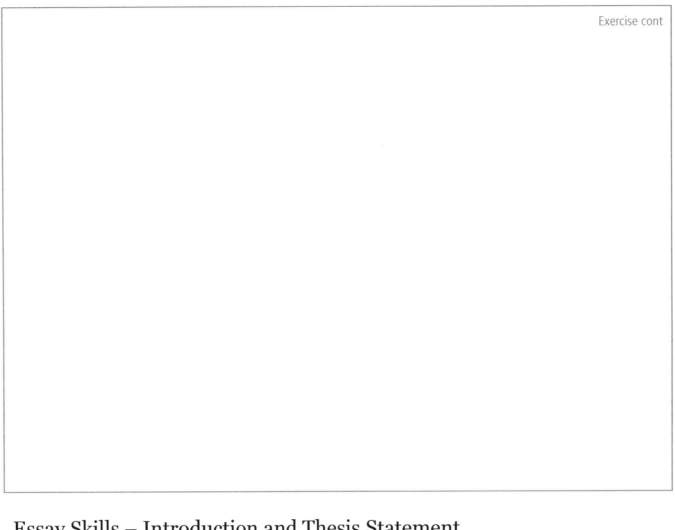

Essay Skills – Introduction and Thesis Statement

Your introduction should:

1. indicate to the reader that you know what the question is about;

2. demonstrate the parameters of the question giving a sense of the two main sides of the argument; and

3. make clear where the essay will go, giving a clear thesis statement.

Exercise: Take this question: 'The principle of love is sufficient to live a good life.' Discuss.

Write an introduction making all three parts of the introduction clear and distinct. One sentence is enough for each, but make sure each sentence is clear and concise.

1. Definition and context: Identify what the question is about and the situation ethics position.

2. Parameters and opposition: State the opposing position, the position of Tillich, for example, that love needs defining in context of justice and forgiveness etc.

3. Thesis statement: Make it clear where you stand, yes, no or somewhere between. Be concise, outlining what your position is.

Christian Moral Action

Structure of Thought

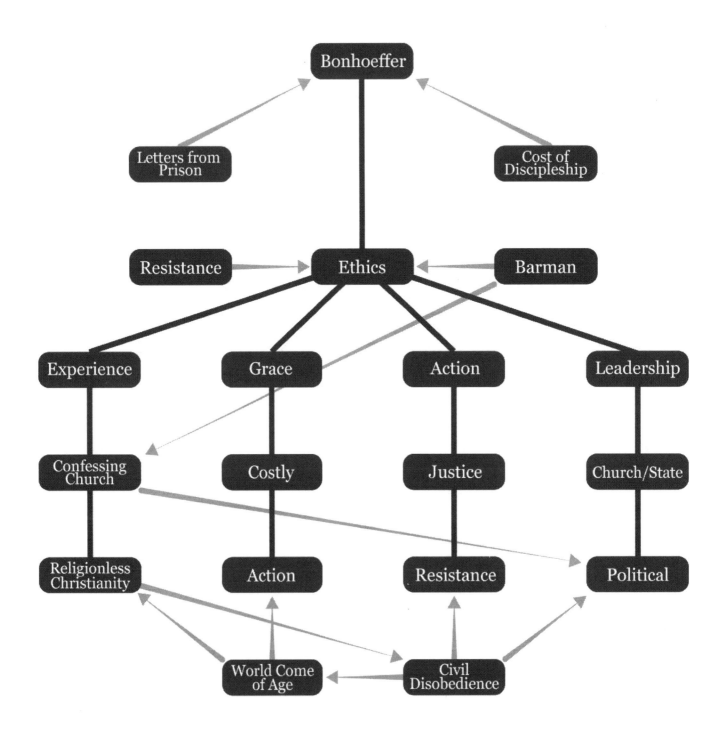

The Teaching and Example of Dietrich Bonhoeffer

Bonhoeffer taught that we do have a responsibility to the state, but this does not mean blind obedience – it means ensuring the state acts according to God's will. The state can never perfectly represent God's will and so can never adopt ultimate power. The Church's role is to keep the state in check – not be a part of it.

In Nazi Germany, the Church was fooled into believing Nazism was bringing order to a disordered society. Christian duty is to disobey the state if it is not acting according to God's will.

Exercise: Bonhoeffer taught that, with regards to obeying the state, we should ask if this is God's will and this would only be clear in the moment of action and as an act of faith. How helpful are the following teachings in helping a Christian to follow Bonhoeffer's teaching?

1. *"You can only know what obedience is by obeying. It is no use asking questions; for it is only through obedience that you come to learn the truth"* (Dietrich Bonhoeffer, The Cost of discipleship, 1959, p. 68)

2. *"There is no road to faith or discipleship, no other road – only obedience to the call of Jesus"* (Dietrich Bonhoeffer, The Cost of discipleship, 1959, p. 49)

Bonhoeffer's teachings could be used to justify civil disobedience. Christian ethics direct us to act out of love – meaning an obligation to challenge injustice.

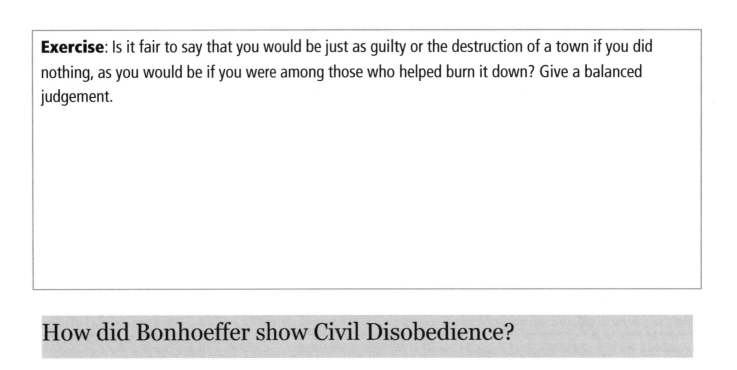

Exercise: Is it fair to say that you would be just as guilty or the destruction of a town if you did nothing, as you would be if you were among those who helped burn it down? Give a balanced judgement.

How did Bonhoeffer show Civil Disobedience?

Bonhoeffer spoke against Nazism in his university position and spoke openly about his prayers for the defeat of his own country. Bonhoeffer also criticised the Confessing Church when it wavered under pressure from Hitler to conform. He went so far as to proclaim Hitler as the Anti-Christ, calling for his elimination. Lastly, Bonhoeffer worked as a double agent with the resistance and the allies, helping to smuggle Jews into Switzerland.

The teaching and example of Dietrich Bonhoeffer on the Church as community and source of spiritual discipline showed a similarity to Kant, Bonhoeffer taught that a Christian can recognise they act out of duty when they act along with the rest of humankind. Bonhoeffer called for a 'religionless Christianity'.

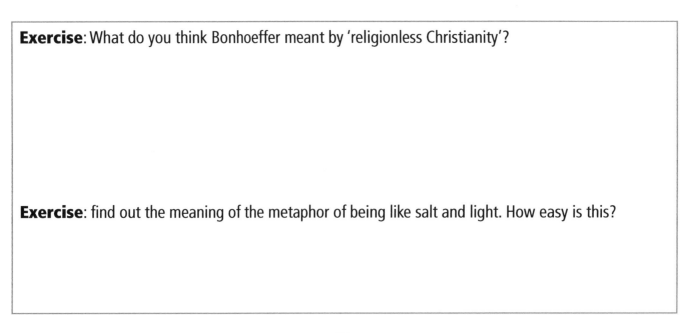

Exercise: What do you think Bonhoeffer meant by 'religionless Christianity'?

Exercise: find out the meaning of the metaphor of being like salt and light. How easy is this?

Bonhoeffer's Role in the Confessing Church

A response to Hitler's decree in 1934 that made it necessary for all clergy to be of Aryan descent. Bonhoeffer and Niemoellar brought together people who disagreed and formed the Confessing Church.

Exercise: The Confessing church met in Barmen and Barth's 'Barmen Declaration' was formed. What was this?

The Confessing Church disagreed with Nazi National socialism and from this, came Bonhoeffer's ecumenical theology. There were to be no national, racial or political boundaries in this 'religionless Christianity' proposed.

Bonhoeffer's Religious Community at Finkenwalde

The key elements of this community which was shut down by the Nazis in 1937, were discipline, meditation, community for others, the Bible and brotherhood.

Ethics as Action: Dietrich Bonhoeffer - Cost of Discipleship

Christianity should not be seen as 'otherworldly' – it is grounded in the everyday world. We should be asking 'who is Christ for us today?' rather than debating issues of his human or divine nature. The meaning of Christianity is seen in its action (Karl Barth). While Barth says God chooses to reveal Himself to us, Bonhoeffer says it is not enough to simply 'receive' the law, we must 'do' the law to. In other words, 'hear' and 'act'.

Costly Grace

The three fundamentals of authentic Christianity are Christ, Scripture and faith. Straying from these would mean nothing but human intervention and religion as an institution is a result of this.

Exercise: What did Bonhoeffer mean by 'cheap grace'?

Discipleship is described as:

 "costly because it costs man his life, and it is grace because it gives man the only true life … Above all, it is costly because it cost God the life of his Son" (The Cost of Discipleship, p. 5).

The Cross is symbolic of Jesus' suffering and in this suffering, Christianity also engages with the world. Discipleship means adopting the Cross and accepting that suffering and sacrifice are an inherent aspect of the nature of discipleship.

Bonhoeffer called for solidarity with the Jews and similarly, living the Christian life is not 'to become religious' but to be there for other people – to be in solidarity with others and to share in their experiences.

Exercise: Do you think Bonhoeffer placed too much emphasis on suffering? Sort the following arguments into 'yes' and 'no' responses and make a judgement.

1. Bonhoeffer's own experience of suffering is not representative of all Christian experience.

2. Bonhoeffer seems to downplay the joy and hope offered by the Resurrection. Jesus' Passion reaches beyond his suffering – the Resurrection represents a triumph over death and sin.

3. Passing through the cross rather than trying to avoid the suffering, is a necessary part of following the call of Jesus.

4. Everyone experiences suffering in some form at some point in their lives.

5. It seems impossible to live a Christian life of discipleship involving suffering and sacrifice if you live in a place of peace and justice.

6. Bonhoeffer's teaching on suffering and discipleship is dependent on injustice and suffering existing.

7. Bonhoeffer focuses on solidarity as well as suffering – people might feel consolation as a result of this.

Essay Skills

Types of Questions

Questions on this topic might focus on Bonhoeffer's teachings on duty to God and state, the church as community and source of spiritual discipline, or on the cost of discipleship.

Whichever it asks, candidates should always use the other in evaluation. Some examples of questions you might be asked are these:

Q. To what extent does the theology of Bonhoeffer have relevance for Christians today?

A. Relevance of solidarity with the poor in today's world and place of Christianity as a 'spiritual conscience' vs idea that obedience to God's rather than the state's law could lead to more conflict than good.

Q. "Christians should practise civil disobedience." Discuss.

A. Critically assess Bonhoeffer's arguments in favour of civil disobedience when the state is going against God's law – how practical is this? Will this lead to more peace or conflict? How can we know that civil disobedience is what God commands? Link to Jesus' teaching on paying taxes to Caesar.

Q. "Bonhoeffer's most important teaching is on leadership." Discuss.

A. Consider leadership in the context of duty to God and duty to state. Assess extent to which other teachings are more important e.g. on the cost of discipleship.

Q. How successful was Bonhoeffer's religious community at Finkenwalde?

A. Define what would make it 'successful' i.e. did it make a stand against Nazism/ or is it successful if it reflects Bonhoeffer's ideas on costly grace and sacrifice? Consider whether the goals at Finkenwalde were in line with Christian teaching and whether they were they practical. What limitations were there?

Exercise: Analyse this question: 'To what extent does Bonhoeffer place too much emphasis on suffering?'

Essay Skills – Introductions and Thesis Statement

Your introduction should:

1. indicate to the reader that you know what the question is about;

2. demonstrate the parameters of the question giving a sense of the two main sides of the argument; and

3. make clear where the essay will go, giving a clear thesis statement.

Exercise: Take this question: 'Bonhoeffer has little relevance today.' Discuss.

Write an introduction making all three parts of the introduction clear and distinct. One sentence is enough for each, but make sure each sentence is clear and concise.

1. Definition and context: Identify what the question is about and the position of solidarity with the poor.

2. Parameters and opposition: State the opposing position, the position of some who would say it would lead to more conflict.

3. Thesis statement: Make it clear where you stand, with yes, no, or somewhere between. Assessing relevance with global politics and plural moral and faith societies could also be relevant in the body of the essay. Be concise, outlining what your position is.

Pluralism - Theology

What is Theological Pluralism?

- Many viewpoints – no overarching narrative or worldview which we can all agree on

- Many religious traditions within Christianity

- Many different religions co-existing

- The argument that Christianity is not the only way to God (Inclusivism)

Religious Pluralism

Religious Pluralism can be viewed diagrammatically as a number of views stretching between two 'poles'

We need to understand the two 'poles', naive realism and critical realism, and then some shades in between.

Naïve realism ————————————————————————————————Critical realism

Harry Gensler ————————————————————————————————John Hick

Naïve Realism

Naive realism is particularly strong in USA where numerous court cases have been fought over whether creationism and/or Darwinism can be taught in schools. Harry Gensler, respected author, signed the Chicago Statement on Biblical Inerrancy in 1978.

- Holds that the Bible is inerrant in its original manuscripts (no errors)

- The Bible is infallible (cannot fail) in its ability to show forth God's will, purpose, commandments, and by extension doctrines such as the divinity and atonement of Christ.

- The Bible should be believed when it speaks about scientific things (7 day creation) and also moral things (homosexual behaviour is a sin, so is pre-marital sex). Key passages: Romans 1:26-7, I Corinthians 6:18 – which has a synoptic link with sexual ethics.

Problems with Naive Realism

- Little understanding about the formation of the Bible, as it was created in a process lasting 500 years – the so-called 'canon' of authoritative books.

- Doesn't seem to acknowledge that categories such as 'scientific' and 'historical' cannot be applied to a document that predates 'science' and 'history' as disciplines.

- Doesn't appear to understand how oral stories are transmitted and then their meaning alters in transmission. Earliest gospel (Mark) written in about 70 AD, about 34 years after Jesus' death. John was written about 90 AD, about 54 years after Jesus' death. How do we know 'Jesus wept?' or 'Lazarus rose again'? Two comments not in Mark, but in John?

- Can't handle contradiction. There are no resurrection appearances in Mark, for example. Mark has one young man in the empty tomb, in the gospel of John, two angels (John 20:12). Mary meets Jesus in John, and thinks he's the gardener. In Mark, Jesus has already 'gone ahead' to Galilee 'there you will see him'.

- The explanation by inerrantists seems like 'death by a thousand qualifications'. They say Mary took multiple trips to the tomb. Dinosaurs lived at the time of Adam, or were put there as fossils to test our faith.

Exercise: Summarise the naive realist view of the statement in John from the lips of Jesus: "I am the way, the truth and the life'.

Hick's Universal Pluralism

A critical realist view, as it takes into accounts the history of Biblical interpretation, what we know from science and also attempts to answer the moral and theological problem – how will God judge people of other faiths? Hick's view is inclusivist – all religions lead to God and reflect aspects of God's truth.

	Hick	Chicago Statement 1978
Assumptions	Literalist readings of the Bible put people off	Literalist readings necessary to be true to Scripture and nature of revelation
Bible	Contains varieties of truth including myth and nn-propositional truth	Primary revelation is propositional and Bible speaks as history and science where relevant
Church	Shrinking so message needs re-interpretation	Churches grow where 'truth' is proclaimed
Culture	Cultural Relativism	Absolutism - claims to historical accuracy
Influences	Kant - truth is mediated by human minds	Holy Spirit mediates absolute truth with authority

Cultural Relativism

"Given the various cultural ways of being human we can ,I think, to some extent understand how it is that they constitute different "lenses" through which the divine Reality is differently perceived" (John Hick).

Hick opposes any view that does not imply absolute truth – one meaning from Bible verses which doesn't change, "For we know that all human awareness involves an indispensable contribution by the perceiver" (John Hick).

Hick claims Kant as his inspiration - the mind is active in perception, organising the impacts of the environment we inhabit on or senses by categories such as cause and effect, time etc.

Hick argues:

"During the last hundred years or so we have been making new observations and have realised

that there is a deep devotion to God, true sainthood, and deep spiritual life within these other religions...would it not be more realistic now to make the shift from Christianity at the centre to God at the centre?" (John Hick)

He sees some truth contained in all religions (so he is inclusivist).

Religious experience, to Hick, suggests a journey from 'self-centredness to reality-centredness' by 'different ways of thinking, feeling and experiencing within the worldwide human family'.

Exercise: Is Hick's argument a form of relativism?

Naive Realism - Absolutism

The naive realist of the Chicago Statement, 1978, has a particular view of literature and history – history is about 'facts' and literature here is a special 'faith witness' from eyewitness accounts by the particular sets of concepts embedded in particular consciousnesses.

There is one, pure meaning which is not culturally relative in any way, but Christocentric, meaning Christ-centred, focusing on the. special revelation of God's unique son who 'emptied himself and 'took the form of a servant', (Philippians 4:12).

Jesus fulfils all messianic prophecy and died as a ransom for our sins (Mark 10:45).

We may ask, however, about behaviour - surely this ought to produce some noticeable difference in our lives?

Christians ought to be better human beings than those who lack these inestimable spiritual benefits

The inerrantists believe that, fired by the Holy Spirit, Christians show the fruits of God's grace in works of sacrificial love. We might link this to situation ethics (even though the naive realist is an ethical absolutist because we need to obey God's commandments unconditionally and read them literally).

Christianity is unique in arguing for the incarnation of a special divine son at one moment in history. To access this truth we must be born again (John 3.16) - a moment of conversion, repentance and faith marks Christians out and sets them apart. Jesus is 'the way, the truth and the life' (John 14:6) and "no-one comes to the Father except through me". Notice inerrantists have a high Christology and emphasises the exalted Lordship of Christ over all creation.

Thought Points

Exercise: research the links between the above ideas and:

1. The anaphatic and cataphatic ways of speaking about God

2. Rahner's idea of the anonymous Christian

3. Kantian ethics

4. John Hick and Feminism – God as verb in feminism

Sources

Hick, J God has Many names

Hick, J in McGrath A. A Christian theology Reader section 9.9

Is Redemptoris Missio Exclusivist or Inclusivist?

Catholic tradition

- God wants everyone to be saved. He "desires all men to be saved and to come to the knowledge of the truth" (1 Tim 2:4).

- Those who seek wholeheartedly to know the good and do it, taking advantage of whatever they have been given, are "substantially joined" to Christ and the Church.

- Pope Pius XII talks about an 'unconscious but intense wish' everyone shares to know God.

- While grace is available in some measure to all, the complete set of goods which God has provided for our salvation, including every means of grace, is available only within the Church.

Lumen Gentium (Vatican II)

This encyclical makes three important points and represents a shift in Catholic thinking:

- Islam and Judaism share a belief in monotheism with Christianity, the church 'regards with esteem' these faiths, and, "Nor is God far distant from those who in shadows and images seek the unknown God, for it is He who gives to all men life and breath and all things, and as Saviour wills that all men be saved."

- "Those also can attain to salvation who through no fault of their own do not know the Gospel of Christ or His Church, yet sincerely seek God'. So anyone who is a genuine seeker may be saved.

- "But often men, deceived by the Evil One, have become vain in their reasonings and have exchanged the truth of God for a lie". This follows the teaching of Paul in Romans 1 (applied there to homosexual practices).

- Redemptoris Missio stresses both proclamation of the gospel and interfaith dialogue. Proclamation is based on the exclusivist claim that human beings can only be saved through Christ and his Church but at the same time, truths are contained in other faiths. Yet the mission itself needs to be 'dialogical' - it needs to take into account that the "hearers of the word" are not just passive receivers.

- Forms of dialogue include:

  - Praying together
  - Neighbourliness
  - Joint projects
  - Joint study
  - Preaching the gospel

Evaluation of Redemptoris Missio

This is a soft exclusivism in contrast with evangelical Christianity's hard exclusivism. The Catholic Church argues that you are only saved by Christ through the church – but other religions and honest seekers will be included in God's salvation plan. The Church consistently attacks 'the relativism of religious pluralism"

Dominus Iesus (2000) states:" All, both Christians and the followers of other religious traditions, are invited by God to enter in the mystery of his patience, as human beings seek his light and truth. Only God knows the times and stages of the fulfilment of this long human quest" (No. 84).

This was a paradigm shift in the 1960s – compare with 1442 CE, words of Pope Eugene IV in "Cantate Domino" which stated:

"The most Holy Roman Church firmly believes, professes and preaches that none of those existing outside the Catholic Church, not only pagans, but also Jews, heretics and schismatics, can have a share in life eternal; but that they will go into the eternal fire which was prepared for the devil and his angels, unless before death they are joined with Her." (Cantate Domino, 1442)

Compare a more recent encyclical:

"The Spirit, then, who is at work in other religions, and supremely in Christ himself, is one and the same Spirit who gives life to the Church." Nostra Aetate 73

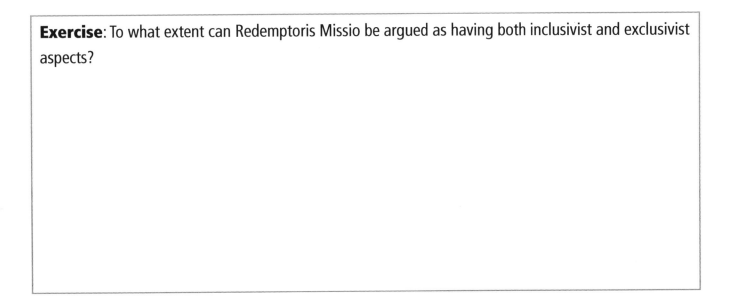

Exercise: To what extent can Redemptoris Missio be argued as having both inclusivist and exclusivist aspects?

What is the Scripture and Reason Movement?

- Shares RC view that the three monotheistic faiths have common ground and all come from the same Old Testament (Hebrew Bible) root.

- Is an example of interfaith dialogue.

- Started as a Jewish movement in the USA in 1990s.

Is Rahner's Anonymous Christian View the same as Hick's?

It's interesting to compare Rahner and Hick. Hick argues:

"Each concrete historical divine personality— Jahweh, the heavenly Father, the Qur`anic Allah--is a joint product of the universal divine presence and a particular historically formed mode of constructive religious imagination." (1993:159)

Theme	Rahner	Hick
Emphasis	Christ -incarnation is God's final revelation in history	God is the 'eternal reality' - The Real. Ultimately unknowable - lives in Kant's inaccessible noumenal realm. "Jesus" becomes anonymous. Experience of the divine becomes the key.
`Other religions	Contain elements of insight but also 'depravity'	Show forth elements of divinity and divine truth
Followers of other faiths	Seekers after truth are 'anonymous Christians'.	Analogy of the sun -all planets reflect something of the one sun's light.
Jesus	Unique Son of God attested by miracles and fulfilled prophecy	Son of God is metaphor meaning Jesus behaved in a godly - not divine and never said he was
Church	Visible symbol of God's presence but Gd also present elsewhere	Church is not sole source of salvation and has no privileged position as guardian of special truth
Christianity	Superior and absolute but God active in pre-history as well	Just one of many ways to God, none superior. Followers of other faiths lead impressive, godly lives.

Hick's Theory: Two Empirical (provable) Statements and Two Assumptions

The Empirical Facts

1. that people are inherently religious

2. the observation that there is substantial diversity in the actual content of religious belief

The Assumptions

3. the assumption that religious belief is not an illusion

4. the assumption that almost every religious tradition positively changes its followers' lives (impossible to prove, and unlikely)

"Exclusivism has what are to some of us unacceptable implications. To put it graphically, consider the analogy of the solar system, with God as the sun at the centre and the religions as the planets circling around that centre. Inclusivism then holds that the life-giving warmth and light of the sun falls directly only on our earth, the Christian church, and is then reflected off it in lesser degrees to the other planets, the other religions." Hick (internet reference online)

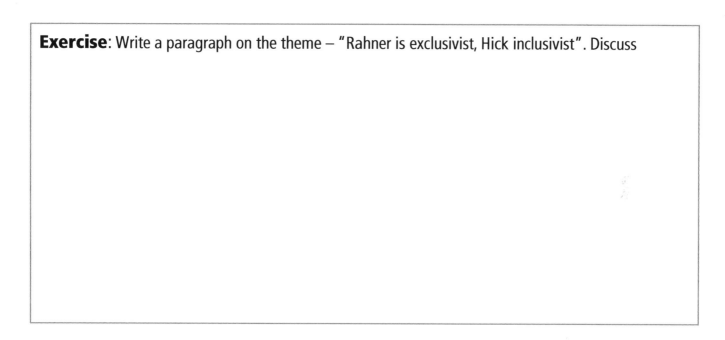

Exercise: Write a paragraph on the theme – "Rahner is exclusivist, Hick inclusivist". Discuss

Essay Skills

Essay title: To what extent can non-Christians who live morally good lives and genuinely seek God be considered to be 'anonymous Christians'?

Answer: The idea of an 'anonymous Christian' arose in the line of thought of Karl Rahner. Rahner argued that Christianity sets the standard by which other religions should be measured; but an omnibenevolent God should be able to extend salvation to those unable to freely accept Christ. He argued that Christ could be followed 'unknowingly' and those with no knowledge of Christ could still have a relationship with God. These people, he would call 'anonymous Christians' However, others such as Handrik Kraemer have argued that non-Christian religions are not responses to God's revelation through Christ and so are cultural constructs rather than a real relationship with God. It seems that the concept of an 'anonymous Christian' might just be trying to label as 'Christian' someone who simply strives for moral goodness. The difficulty in labelling them as anonymously Christian is that such people may not even seek God, and openly reject Christ.

Exercise: Try and Opening Paragraph on this essay title.

"All religions lead to God". Discuss with reference to both inclusivist and exclusivist claims.

Further Reading

John Hick's Pluralistic Hypothesis by Keith Johnson (online)

Religious Pluralism and Islam by John Hick (online)

Gender and Theology (Society)

Forms of Feminism

- Radical feminism

- Post-Christian feminism

- Liberal feminism

Sources of Patriarchy

1. Natural Law - "God is sovereign over his Creation. The covenant of nature has not been annulled but re-established in the covenant of grace by which Christ as head rules his people as obedient servants. Male and female, then, are necessarily ordered in a relation of those who lead and those who follow. Men and women should accept their own place in this order, the man humbly and the woman willingly." Karl Barth

2. Bible – "I do not permit a woman to have authority over a man". St Paul (1 Timothy 2:12)

3. Church – after Constantine's conversion in 312 the Church becomes organ of a hierarchical state (Prince Bishops emerge later in the UK)

4. Biology – Aristotle "women are misbegotten males" (On the Parts of Animals, ii, 3) Aquinas "in man the discretion of reason predominates".

"It is idolatrous to make males more 'like God' than females. It is blasphemous to use the image and name of the Holy to justify patriarchal domination and law. Feminist readings of the Bible can discern a norm within Biblical faith by which the Biblical texts themselves can be criticised. To the extent to which Biblical texts reflect this normative principle, they are regarded as authoritative." (Ruether, Sexism and God-talk page 48)

Hermeneutics of Ephesians 5:22-33

We can note that only in the Christian Thought paper can you get a bible passage actually mentioned in the exam question (because it's in the actual specification, not the suggested reading which I have placed in brackets in the table in an earlier section).

What might these questions look like?

With reference to the parable of the sheep and the goats (Matthew 25:31-46) assess the view that people will be condemned to hell for their actions.

Using Matthew 25:31-46, critically assess the evidence that Christians believe hell to be a physical place.

With reference to Mark 6:47-52 and John 9:1-41, what grounds are there for arguing Jesus thought of himself as a divinely-anointed Messiah?

"Jesus was just a teacher of wisdom". Discuss, with reference to Matthew 5:17-48.

"Jesus Christ was a revolutionary liberator". Assess this view with reference to Mark 5:24-34.

Evaluate the view that Paul's teachings are the origin of sexism, with reference to Ephesians 5:22-33.

Let's be clear: all these are quite fair and legitimate questions. Let's also be clear: few students are equipped to handle this sort of question. The reason is this: returning to my second integrating principe of hermeneutics, there is no guidance in the specification about how to interpret Scripture and evaluate big questions arising out of so-called literal readings of these chapters. So here are some suggestions.

1. Link these passages to religious pluralism and try to understand the mindset of the literalist or fundamentalist interpretation which is exemplified by statements such as the Chicago Declaration on Biblical Inerrancy 1978. then contrast this with the liberal interpretations which might be inspired by Bultmann on myth, or Hick on universal pluralism. You will see how a variety of readings come out of two different philosophical positions.

2. Try to do a proper case study on these passages and see how they are interpreted by the levels of history I mentioned under integrating principle 1 in an earlier chapter. So take Augustine's reading, Aquinas' reading, Calvin's reading, and compare these to the feminist readings of the same passage (I'm thinking here of Ephesians) or liberationist readings of Matthew 25. By the way, in ten years worshipping in various evangelical churches I never once heard a sermon on Matthew 25 because it appears to teach an evangelical heresy that we are justified (saved) according to our works, not by our faith.

3. Always place Scripture in context. The New Testament needs to be interpreted in the context of the Old Testament, and one verse in the New Testament in the context of the whole book in which it comes. I know it sounds like hard work, but you really need to examine the theology of Matthew to understand Matthew 25, and Paul's whole theology of personhood to understand Ephesians 5. That's if you want to get an A grade on these sorts of questions. Finally the whole Bible needs to be placed in the context of its time. If you want to understand the times of Jesus the best summary I have read is in Ched Myers' book, Binding the Strong Man, a Marxist Reading of Mark. this book is a very useful bridge, too, to liberation theology.

How Might We Handle Ephesians 5?

This book on Christian Thought is not a textbook, but a study guide, hopefully helping you to ask (and answer) the right questions., but because textbooks gloss over the issue of hermeneutics and how we read texts, and how texts are read by different cultures. We can illustrate from Ephesians 5 how the issues arise, and what we might say that isn't naive over-generalisation.

There is a problem however: on a superficial reading, Ephesians 5 does appear to be offensive and sexist to the modern reader:

Wives, submit yourselves to your husbands as you do to the Lord. For the husband is the head of the wife as Christ is the head of the church, his body, of which he is the Saviour. Now as the church submits to Christ, so also wives should submit to their husbands in everything. (Ephesians 5:22-24)

First of all there is the issue of the Greek text itself. The earliest manuscript we have of Paul's letter is the Codex Vaticanus (dated 325 AD), which does not contain the key word 'submit' as in Ephesians 5:22 "wives, submit to your husbands as to the Lord".

Was this key verse therefore a later addition, placed there by church authorities worried about the radicalness of some of Paul's statements? There would also seem to be a 'controlling thought' in this passage - 'submit yourselves to one another out of reverence to Christ' (Ephesians 5:21), which implies a mutual submission to each other in the spirit of sacrificial love, rather than the inferiority of women.

Secondly, notice that this verse (in its later version) fundamentally contradicts Paul's teaching in Galatians: "now therefore, there is neither Jew nor Greek, slave nor free, male nor female, we are all one In Christ Jesus" (Galatians 3:28). There are few more revolutionary statements in the Bible about gender equality than this one. So which is the real Paul? And how does this square with Jesus' very revolutionary attitude to women, shown, for example, in Mark 5 when he addresses the bleeding woman who had just polluted him (blood renders you unclean) by touching his cloak: "daughter, go in peace, your faith has made you well". There is radical inclusion in this word 'daughter'. No wonder Jesus' followers are recorded in Mark a s being 'astonished'.

As we interpret the Bible we have to attempt to reconcile supposedly contradictory statements, otherwise we do neither Paul nor Jesus justice. Or we do what Rosemary Ruether suggests and apply the feminist hermeneutic, and simply reject any passage which demeans, discomforts or denigrates women. This is what we might describe as the feminist lens of interpretation (just as the non-negotiable doctrine of justification by faith supplies a Protestant reformer's lens of interpretation of Matthew 25, the parable of the Sheep and the Goats).

Finally, we need to realise that the interpretations given to this passage by, for example, Augustine, are not 'pure' interpretations, but in his case, clouded by neo-Platonic ideas including those of the fundamental irrationality and inferiority of women. Have modern evangelical interpretations of women's issues simply inherited uncritically Augustine's distortion? Here's what Augustine says, and notice the body/soul dualism here which is transposed onto male/female gender differences:

The apostle puts flesh for woman; because, when she was made of his rib, Adam said, "This is now bone of my bone, and flesh of my flesh." And the apostle says, "He that loves his wife loves himself; for no one ever hated his own flesh." Flesh, then, is put for woman, in the same manner that spirit is sometimes put for husband. Why? Because the one rules, the other is ruled; the one ought to command, the other to serve. For where the flesh commands and the spirit serves, the house is turned the wrong way round. What can be worse than a house where the woman has the mastery over the man? But that house is rightly ordered where the man commands and the woman obeys. In like manner that man is rightly ordered where the spirit commands and the flesh serves. (Augustine, On John Tractate 2, section 14)

Notice that Augustine argues that just as the spirit is superior to the body, so the husband, even though he is flesh, is superior to the woman. It's a strange and twisted piece of logic but the end result is Augustine's conclusion: a house is rightly ordered where a man commands and a woman obeys.

What has happened here is that neo-Platonic categories and dualisms have filtered Augustine's interpretation, just as prejudices about women pre-filter (arguably) how evangelical Christians seem to read the Bible. Or so would be my argument, the point being, we need to discuss how these texts are interpreted and consider whether the superficial interpretation, or the historical one of Augustine quoted above, is actually correct. And what principles drive their sometimes very different interpretations.

Our conclusion is that the traditional reading is actually a patriarchal reading of Ephesians which rejects the radical, liberating idea of mutual submission in Christian marriage. It insists that just as Jesus was the Lord and Master of the church, so too must a husband be lord and master of his wife. In other words, according to patriarchal theology, it is the "lordship" of Jesus that husbands are told to imitate in marriage.

But is this the thrust of Paul's argument? It would seem not: his argument is based on the equality principle of considering one another's interests above your own, the agape principle in Chris's example of outpouring and giving love. It's easy to miss this fundamental point if you selectively quote Ephesians 5:22, a text that may well be a later insertion by the church. These are the issues underlying the concept of the two horizons of hermeneutics introduced by Hans-Georg Gadamer to clarify the issues involved in interpretation, the horizon of the text and the horizon of our own time and culture.

Exercise: How did Augustine's culture and neo-Platonism affect and bias his interpretation of Ephesians 5?

Structure of Thought – Rosemary Ruether, Liberal Feminist

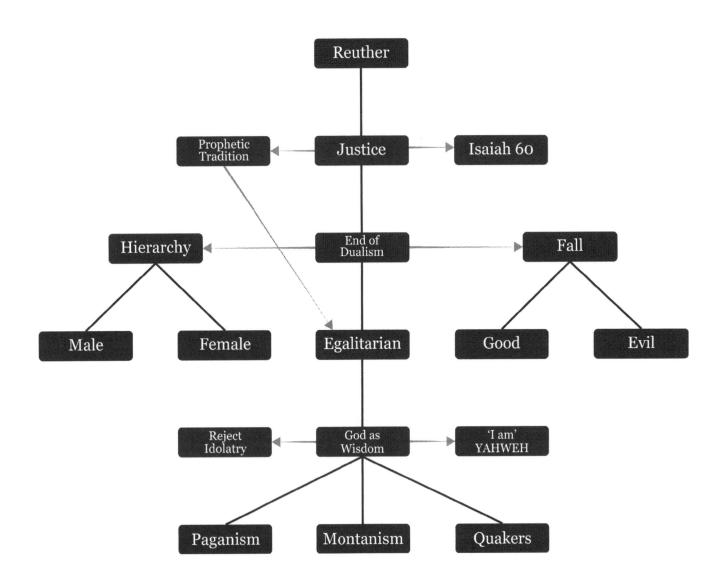

Hermeneutic of Suspicion

Feminist hermeneutic is critical of Scripture – Ruether takes the Exodus model as the defining story (Jewish people cross the Red Sea and escape from slavery in Egypt) and sees Galatians 3:28 (neither male, nor female but all one in Christ) as the expression of this in the New Testament. This implies three things:

- The Bible is not all the word of God (it contains God's word, but also contains the words of humans which reflect their world view).

- Interpretations are not neutral but are subjective and contextual

- Feminist theology should be done from the starting point of experience

The Prophetic-liberating Tradition – Justice

- A golden thread in the Bible

- Equality (as in Galatians 3:28 'there is neither male nor female')

- Names of God need to reflect the inclusiveness of the message

God/ess Theology

- 'God/ess' figure is venerated as the female principle of existence and source of life but without the same degree of patriarchal hierarchy of monotheism.

- though Christianity is monotheistic, it has never lost its ancient roots in the Goddess and polytheism

- God/ess influences suppressed by early church - 'For a long time I have held my peace I have kept still and restrained myself, now I will cry out like a woman in labour, I will gasp and pant.' Isaiah 42:14

Wisdom

- *'For wisdom is more mobile than any motion; because of her pureness she pervades and penetrates all things. For she is a breath of the power of God, and a pure emanation of the glory of the Almighty; therefore nothing defiled gains entrance into her. For she is a reflection of eternal light, a spotless mirror of the working of God'. Wisdom of Solomon 7:24-26 (Apocrypha)*

- Greek Sophia – always female

- Challenges the gender dualism of the Bible

'Because God is our king, we need obey no human kings. Because God is our parent, we are liberated from dependence on patriarchal authority.' (Rosemary Radford Ruether, Sexism and God-Talk, page 55)

Jesus Christ

- Early Christians made the connection between sophia and Jesus Christ.

- Jesus as divine wisdom explained his relationship to God, his identity on earth and the source of his teaching.

- St Paul, 'We proclaim Christ crucified... to those who are called, both Jews and Greeks, Christ the power of God and the wisdom of God' (1 Corinthians 1:23-24).

- John's Gospel. Christ = eternal wisdom but uses the Greek equivalent term logos (meaning 'word') because of the maleness of the historical Jesus. As Logos, God created the universe (John 1:1-3) and then was incarnated in the form of Jesus (John 1:14).

- "Most of all, images of God/ess must be transformative, pointing us back to our authentic potential and forward to new redeemed possibilities". Ruether

> **Exercise**: How does Rosemary Ruether interpret the idea of Messiah and the gender of Jesus?

Can a Male Saviour Save?

- Jesus Christ is not only historically male but as the Word or Logos of God he is also the male. For a woman to be saved would mean denying the kind of person she is and adapting herself to a male mind-set.

- Salvation is about entry into the Kingdom of God as place or state after death. Entry is competitive, hierarchical and dependent on keeping to church duties. For a woman to be saved would mean wanting to enter into a male dominated church organisation.

- But Jesus' life and ministry rejects the Davidic kingly warrior messiah role.

- The Kingdom of God was not about having worldly power but gaining justice and dignity for the marginalised. Ruether is a Liberation Theologian.

- The Kingdom is not an afterlife reward but healing and restoring all human relationships now. Realised eschatology (the end times come now).

- So….Jesus' gender is irrelevant to his saving role, argues Ruether.

Exercise: Write an opening paragraph on the question "Can a male saviour save?"

Mary Daly – Radical Feminist (Leave the Church)

"Patriarchy is a society manufactured and controlled by males. Fatherland. A society in which every legitimated institution is entirely in the hands of males, and a few selected henchwomen. A society which is characterised by oppression, repression, depression, narcissism, cruelty, racism, classism, ageism, speciesism, objectification, sadomasochism, necrophilia, joyless society ruled by Godfather, Son and Company; society fixated on proliferation, propagation, procreation and bent on the destruction of all life." (Mary Daly, Gyn-ecology)

Assumptions

1. Teleological assumption – the purpose is liberation from oppression.

   "Some biblical material that appears not to address women, or even appears hostile to them, can be reworked to bring out liberating themes for abused women….Consciousness-raising for these women has provided the essential catalyst: the insight that women are included in the category of the poor, the oppressed, and the outcast." (Letty Russell (1985:102)

2. Feminist theology assumes patriarchy infects all biblical thinking in the early church, because all the evidence available suggest the church was patriarchal. So we need to disentangle the patriarchal tradition from the Bible (Ruether) or we reject the Bible altogether (Daly, Hampson).

3. Experience is the key to good hermeneutics:

   "Whatever diminishes or denies the full humanity of women must be presumed not to reflect the divine or an authentic relation to the divine, to reflect the authentic nature of things, or to be the message or work of an authentic redeemer or a community of redemption.' (Ruether, Sexism and God-Talk).

Daly agrees.

Compare Ruether and Daly

	Mary Daly	Rosemary Ruether
Hermeneutic	Suspicion of existing structures/ deconstruction of the patriarchal worldview evidence in hierarchy, theology and language	Suspicion of existing structures/ recovery of lost or suppressed traditions – must be true to women's **experience**
Patriarchy	Is the 'foreground' of society governing structures of power and attitudes to women	Exists in the structures of thought and power which need to be replaced by the new incarnation/ theology
Church	Primary purveyor of patriarchy with its processional priests and necrophiliac doctrine and so must be abandoned forever for a new community	Primary purveyor of patriarchy in its theology of male headship and the masculine God but women remain there to transform it
God	Portrayed as a reflection of male imagination and fantasy with women as submissive virgin (good) or (evil) whore. Sees God as elemental life-force of the Universe - **Quintessence**.	Portrayed as King, Lord or Warrior, needs transforming into genderless source of wisdom and justice – "I am" divine presence/ **Wisdom**
Jesus	Rejected as part of the hierarchy of males in the godhead and irrelevant to women	Rediscovered as the incarnation of the wisdom of God whose gender is irrelevant. "Word became flesh'. John 1
Women	Need to embody the biophilic life and reject the necrophiliac, rapist, dominant culture of patriarchy	Become prophets of the new eschatological order and embody values of equality and justice
Men	Irredeemably part of the patriarchal structures and incapable of being saved from it	Redeemable within the new dispensation of justice and peace
Summary	Radical, post-Christian. Inspirations – Simone de Beauvoir and second wave feminism and Paul Tillich	Radical Christian – inspirations paganism, heresy such as Montanism, early feminists

Evaluation

Exercise: Here are some quotes on feminism taken from Christian Thought – Revision Guide. Take one quote and evaluate whether you agree or disagree, using the word 'because' to justify your view.

1. "It is idolatrous to make males more 'like God' than females. It is blasphemous to use the image and name of the Holy to justify patriarchal domination and law. Feminist readings of the Bible can discern a norm within Biblical faith by which the Biblical texts themselves can be criticised. To the extent to which Biblical texts reflect this normative principle, they are regarded as authoritative." Ruether, Sexism and Godtalk,(Boston: Beacon Press, 1983:23)

2. "Patriarchy is a society manufactured and controlled by males. Fatherland. A society in which every legitimated institution is entirely in the hands of males, and a few selected henchwomen. A society which is characterised by oppression, repression, depression, narcissism, cruelty, racism, classism, ageism, speciesism, objectification, sadomasochism, necrophilia, joyless society ruled by Godfather, Son and Company; society fixated on proliferation, propagation, procreation, and bent on the destruction of all life." Mary Daly

3. "A critical feminist theology of liberation does not speak of male oppressors and female oppressed, of all men over and against all women but about patriarch as a pyramidal system and hierarchical structure of Society and church in which women's oppression is specified, not only in terms of race and class, but also in terms of marital status." E.S. Fiorenza, "Emerging issues in feminist Biblical interpretation" in J.L. Weidman (ed.), Christian feminism: Visions of a new humanity, (San Francisco: Harper & Row, 1984:37).

4. "Indeed, all who seek liberation, women and men, black and white, will ultimately meet on common ground. As women we shall meet in the centre of the circle as issues of rape, battering, economic and sexual exploitation, legal discrimination, pornography and prostitution draw us together." Feminist Liberation Theology A Contextual Option by Denise Ackermann Journal of Theology for Southern Africa, 1988, no. 62, pp.14-28

Essay-writing Skill

Exercise: Taking one short quote from Ruether and one from Daly, write an opening paragraph on this question: "Critically compare the feminist theology of Ruether and Daly".

Example: "Feminists argue the Church is irrevocably sexist". Discuss

Answer: In this essay a contrast and distinction is made between the radical feminist Mary Daly and the Liberal feminist Rosemary Ruether. It will be seen that they share common themes and concerns: the infectious nature of patriarchy, which pollutes all it touches, the importance of women's experience and the search for equality and justice. However, whereas Ruether argues we should transform the Church and the concept of God by critically exposing the prophetic- liberating tradition in the Bible, Daly argues that the tradition is morally bankrupt. Patriarchy has polluted and destroyed the credibility of the Biblical accounts of the God concept and we must now exit the church and form a new charismatic community on principles that reflect the divine essence. The very God-concept needs to change from King and Father to God-ess (Ruether) or Quintessence (Daly).

Secularism – Charles Taylor

"This modern Christian consciousness lives in a tension… between what it draws from the development of modern humanism, and its attachment to the central mysteries of Christian faith'. Charles Taylor A Secular Age, chapter 10

- Programmatic - a programme of removing religion from public life (Dawkins, Freud)

- Procedural - a set of rules and procedures to guarantee freedom of expression (including religion)

Charles Taylor - A Secular Age

"The modern Christian consciousness lives in a tension… between what it draws from the development of modern humanism, and its attachment to the central mysteries of Christian faith'." Charles Taylor, A Secular Age Ch 10

- I did not know death had undone so many" TS Eliot

- Secular 'waste land' - "young people will begin again to explore beyond the boundaries." (p. 770)

- Celebrate the "integrity of different ways of life." (p. 772)

- "Disenchanted age" hungry for meaning

Exercise: Review of A Secular Age - read the review on the next page and list three things that are distinctive about Charles Taylor's approach.

The most searching and original – but also unsettled and unsettling– parts of Taylor's book concern what he calls "Secularism 3 ".

This focuses on "a move from a society where belief in God is unchallenged and indeed, unproblematic, to one in which it is understood to be one option among others, and frequently not the easiest to embrace" (p. 3). Secularism is not just a net reduction in religious belief or practice, therefore, but a change in the very conditions of belief. Taylor is clear that in many ways secularism makes belief harder, but he doesn't see only negatives on the balance sheet. Secularism has come about alongside changes that we should value, like a deeper notion of self and subjective agency and a more egalitarian social order.

Moreover, though belief may be problematic in new ways, it is also possible for it to be meaningful in new ways.

Taylor really means belief. He doesn't want to see religion as just a number of engaging practices or quasi-ethnic customs. It turns centrally on belief in God or at least something larger and perhaps better than mere this-worldly human flourishing that defines religious faith. But Taylor steers clear of some of the common complaints against a belief-centred account of religion. He does not mean belief in specific doctrines. Nor does he understand belief as an abstract intellectual commitment to the truth of a propositional statement.

Rather, he devotes considerable effort to showing how that sort of narrowed "epistemological" approach is part of a package of cultural and intellectual changes that make religious belief hard, even while they make for advances in other domains like science.

We start out with easy access to a sense of fullness, but don't know very well what we have. We grow in knowledge (or as Rousseau would say, in arts and science), but in ways that cut us off from full relationships to nature, our own lives, other people, and God. Yet there is potential for returning to a sense of fullness informed by poetry and philosophy as well as religion.

Making the idea – and experience – of transcendence sensible is one of Taylor's central goals. Acknowledging that religion can be defined in a variety of ways, his interest in it is defined by this – or rather by the relationship between "immanence" and "transcendence". And as importance as transcendence is, most of his book is devoted to trying to understand immanence. Taylor sees the modern West as shaped deeply by the idea of a natural order understandable without reference to anything outside itself (unless perhaps human consciousness is understood this way, though as Taylor notes, it is often understood as one more natural phenomenon). Indeed, he suggests that this is "the great invention of the West" (p. 15). It is constitutive for an "immanent frame" within which one can set aside questions of divine creation, marking off a sharp boundary with the transcendent. The orderliness of the world is now impersonal, perhaps set in motion by a watchmaker- God, but working of itself. (Craig Calhoun (European Journal of Sociology, 49 (03). p. 455.2008)

Enlightenment and Diversity

- Secularism is the Way Democracies deal with Diversity

- Religion retreating

- Religion is one type of belief and practice among many

- A certain kind of metaphysical belief under attack

No Religion Doesn't Mean No Belief

- Humans are embedded in society, society in the cosmos, and the cosmos incorporates the divine." (p. 152)

- But idea of society has changed – from Natural law hierarchy

- To "a salvation which takes us beyond what we usually understand as human flourishing." (p. 152)

- A "a telos of autarky" emerges from Protestant Reformation (p. 138) Individualism

- Distance emerges between God and us – 'buffered self' replaces 'porous self'.

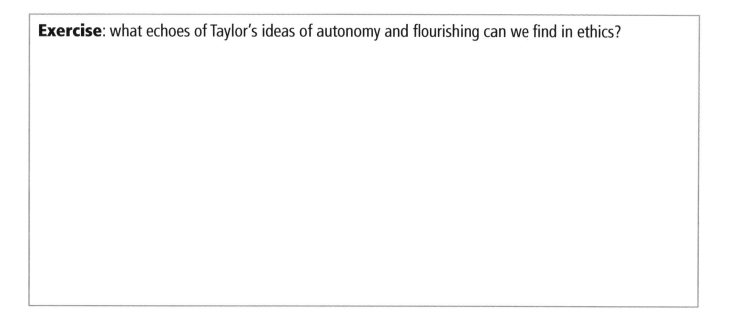

Exercise: what echoes of Taylor's ideas of autonomy and flourishing can we find in ethics?

Thought Point

Charles Taylor's argument 'no religion doesn't mean 'no belief' echoes the research findings of sociologist Linda Woodhead. Following a 2013 Government survey which showed 51% of the UK had 'no religion' she discovered that young people's views especially were out of line with mainstream Christian thinking on things such as sexual morals, gay rights, transgender issues. You can find a summary of her report online at the Journal of the British Academy. She concludes:

This means that whilst a majority of British people now identify as 'nones', and their dominance is set to increase, we cannot accurately describe Britain as 'post-Christian' or straightforwardly non-religious. A yawning values gap has opened between the churches and younger generations, but Christianity remains strongly institutionalised and influential, whilst other religions have grown in influence. Britain is no longer the 'Christian country' the Daily Mail imagines, but neither is it 'no religion'. It exists somewhere in-between—between Christian, multi-faith and 'none'. (Linda Woodhead, Journal of the British Academy, 4, page 245–61, 2016)

Implications of Secularism

- Tolerate each other's values

- Religion private, personal choice 'we don't do religion'

- Experiment in areas such as sexual identity

- Spirituality replaces organised religion

"Seeking a kind of unity and wholeness of the self, of the body and its pleasures. The stress is on unity, integrity, holism, individuality." (p. 507)

Procedural Secularism

The Secular Society argues that procedural secularism is necessary for religious toleration and the freedom and flourishing of all religious life.

US Constitution guarantees freedom of religion, bans religious education in schools. The Establishment Clause of the first amendment states: "Congress shall make no law respecting an establishment of religion".

In 1990 the Webster Supreme Court ruling stated: "If a teacher in a public school uses religion and teaches religious beliefs or espouses theories clearly based on religious underpinnings, the principles of the separation of church and state are violated".

Programmatic Secularism

Richard Dawkins – The God Delusion

- Religious upbringing is a form of child abuse. He implies it's worse than sexual abuse because it permanently damages their thought processes, induces guilt, promotes irrationality, and leads to judgementalism.

- Philomena Lee had her child, born outside marriage removed, and forcibly adopted

- In the empiricist tradition of Hume and the Logical Positivists (AJ Ayer) – existence of God does not stand up to proof and is therefore an irrational delusion

- Religious practices are often harmful eg teaching young children to believe in hell by re-enacting it on stage (US Hell House), disparaging science by teaching creationism, teaching children to feel guilty about sex or their sexual orientation

Evaluation of Dawkins

- Alister McGrath argues Dawkins misrepresents idea of 'faith' as 'blind trust against all evidence'. Christianity means by faith 'a personal relationship, based on experience and in conformity with the metaphysical facts of the world".

- Example – existence of God explains the facts of mystery, beauty, morality and the origin of the Universe. 'What caused the big bang?' is as big a mystery as 'God brought the Universe into existence" or 'who created God?'

- Behaviour – Dawkins assembles a vast evidence of evil or ridiculous religious practices. This is a straw man argument as he sets religion up to be knocked down. It is bad religion not good religion that he is considering.

A Straw Man Argument against Evolution

"Look at how Darwin's theory led to mass sterilisation of disabled and mentally deficient people starting in Michigan in 1897 in the USA, gaining momentum in 33 states in the 1920s. This is in line with eugenics, but against fundamental human rights such as Article 39. Between 1897 and 1981 65,000 women were sterilised. Hitler, inspired by eugenics, forced the same policy on Nazi Germany and then extended it to include murder in the gas chambers. Therefore Darwinism is highly abusive and we should do all we can to eliminate it."

Exercise: What is wrong with the above argument against Darwin's Theory of Evolution?

Sigmund Freud – Future of an Illusion

Freud examines the psychological and social causes for the persistence of religious belief.

1. Social

   Religious belief confirms the status quo in society and reduces unrest. Less privileged citizens believe they are compensated by God in an afterlife. They are encouraged to feel guilty about civil unrest. They are encouraged to believe in a natural divine order for society (as in natural law theory) and in the design of the world (natural philosophy).

2. Psychological

   Religion panders to a psychological need for a father-figure to sort out complexity and right apparent problems with my life. There is an infantile need for order, commands to follow, and purpose. Life is complex and at times baffling.

   Religion creates neurosis by encouraging negative feelings and guilt about sex, sexual orientation and masturbation. It encourages conflict between ego, id and superego and preserves the superego in an infantile state – which stems from our childhood upbringing and parental praise and blame, aged 3-5 years.

Evaluation

- Keith Ward argues this is a form of reductionism – reducing humans to less than we are.

- There is such an idea as mature Christian belief where evidence is weighed and probabilities considered.

- Religion is also a protest movement – link with liberation theology – and not just a means of social control.

- Freud's theory of human consciousness, involving id, ego and superego is another metaphysical hypothesis – it cannot be proved scientifically. Indeed the sample of Freud's own patients (largely hysterical, middle class, female) is not representative

Should Christianity Play no Part in Public Life?

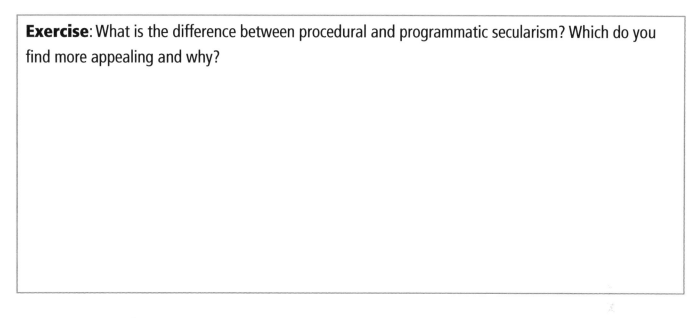

Exercise: What is the difference between procedural and programmatic secularism? Which do you find more appealing and why?

The main aims of humanism were set out in the Amsterdam Declaration of 1952. These aims included ethical and rational approaches, a support of democracy and human rights, the importance of personal liberty and the maximisation of possible human fulfilment.

Keeping Church and state separate has been seen as one way of minimising conflict.

Programmatic secularists believe the government should go further in separating the church and state, but Christopher Dawson has highlighted the challenge that a secular education would deprive people of the chance to make sense of their culture which, to a large extent, has been immersed in religion.

Terry Eagleton proposed an approach to the secularisation model that was both Marxist and Christian. He thought it important to still pay attention to the role played by religious imagination in its contribution to human existence and the harm it causes should be weighed up against its positive contributions. Secularism cannot capture the spiritual aspect of being human, but religion can.

Exercise: Create a list of arguments for and against the accusation that Christianity is a major cause of personal and social problems. Overall, which side of the argument is stronger?

Essay-writing Sample

Exercise: Work on the opening paragraph. Try an opening paragraph on this subject:

"Secularism has destroyed the credibility of religious belief". Discuss

Make sure you have a thesis statement summing up your view and mention the names of Dawkins, Freud and McGrath. The word 'credibility' also needs to be explored and 'secularism' defined.

Example: "Christianity is a delusion'. Discuss

Answer: Christianity is a delusion according to both Dawkins, who uses the word, and Freud who refers to the future of an 'illusion'. Perhaps 'delusion' is more pejorative than 'illusion' as it suggests a kind of irrational madness, whereas Freud's suggestion is more in line with a mirage in the desert. My argument here is that both arguments are a form of reductionism, as they reduce Christianity to something less than it is, and also employ a fallacy known as 'the straw man argument ' to make their case, in which only negative examples are considered. I will also consider the views of Alister McGrath and Keith Ward against Dawkins and Freud.

Liberation Theology and Marx (Challenges)

Structure of Thought

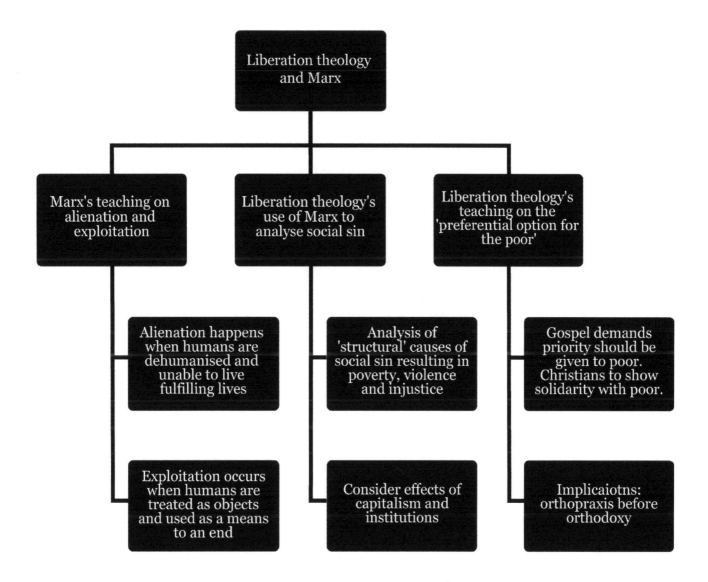

Objectification in Hegel

Marx was inspired by Hegel to take two Hegelian ideas - objectification and alienation - and turn them from an idea concerning human consciousness, to an idea of linked to economic reality, located in unjust structures. For Marx alienation included alienation from the process of work and its rewards. Human beings become 'objectified' and turned into instruments of economic relations. Peter Critchley describes Hegelian thought in this way:

Hegel had a particular way of speaking about the human spirit which involved the use of two of his most important concepts — objectification and alienation. According to Hegel, all human history is a process whereby ideas objectify themselves in material reality. Thus, the idea of 'shelter' is objectified into houses, the ideas of 'communication' and 'transport' are objectified into roads, railways, buses, cars. And the idea of a 'general interest of society' is objectified into the institutions of the state.

However, this process of objectification is also, for Hegel, a process of alienation. Because as mind objectifies itself into innumerable different material products and social and political institutions (the family, the occupational group, the state) it fails to grasp that these things are its products, its embodiments, its manifold objectifications. Hence it treats them as things separate ('alien') from itself. In fact this was how Hegel explained empiricism, empiricism was the expression, in the realm of philosophy, of mind's alienation from itself.

The linked concepts of objectification and alienation bring us to the heart of Hegel's philosophy of history. For Hegel, human history is the process by which mind first alienates itself through objectification and then, gradually and in stages, recognises these objectifications as its own products and comes, therefore, to understand these objectifications and its own achievements and potential.

For Hegel, the goal, the culmination of history is the overcoming of alienation and the final triumph of reason. This consists in mind's total self-understanding and self-consciousness both of itself and thus (simultaneously) of the world. Peter Critchley

Exercise: Explain Hegel's concept of objectification.

Marx's Teaching on Alienation and Exploitation

Alienation was Marx's way of describing the state of humans when left living unfulfilling lives as a result of being 'dehumanised'. This happens when they are exploited and are treated as a means to an end.

This idea helps us to think about the people involved in the production of things we value.

Exercise: Think of something you bought recently. How many different human roles in production can you identify? Do you think it is important to know this?

Marx would say we should not just see people as a means of production, which 'objectifies' them.. The more developed the technology, the less in control we feel. We are able to produce surplus to requirements but this favours those who control the means of production – there is a human cause to class division. Marx's criticism of capitalism lay in his observation that private ownership changed transformed the relationship between people and the means of production.

Exercise: What is the social issue Marx has identified? How might it be tackled? Do you see it present today? Do you think religion can have a role in tackling it?

Liberation Theology's use of Marx to Analyse Social Sin

Liberation theology began as both a theological and a practical movement. Gustavo Gutiérrez proposed that liberation occurs both social and economic – from poverty and oppression, and from sin. These aspects must happen together.

Exercise: How might Matthew 25:40 considered in the (Death and the Afterlife section) have influenced liberation theology?

Liberation theology focused on the development of human well-being rather than wealth.

This links to Marx's observation that industrialisation can sacrifice human wellbeing. Liberation theology links a 'structure of sin' to this industrialisation process.

Exercise: Gutiérrez suggested that being Christian necessitated being political. What are arguments in favour of this and what are arguments against? What do you think?

Exercise: Consider the following extracts. How might each of them relate to Marxist ideas and the ideas of liberation theology?

1. "The growth of the Kingdom is a process which occurs historically in liberation, insofar as liberation means a greater fulfilment of man" (Gutiérrez, A Theology of Liberation, 1973, p. 177).

2. "Then the LORD said to Moses, "Go to Pharaoh and say to him, 'This is what the LORD, the God of the Hebrews, says: "Let my people go, so that they may worship me." (Exodus 9:1).

3. He has performed mighty deeds with his arm; he has scattered those who are proud in their inmost thoughts. He has brought down rulers from their thrones but has lifted up the humble. He has filled the hungry with good things but has sent the rich away empty. (Luke 1:51-53)

4. Again I tell you, it is easier for a camel to go through the eye of a needle than for someone who is rich to enter the kingdom of God." (Matthew 19:24).

A Preferential Option for the Poor

The Christian duty to prioritise the poor and act in solidarity with them is demanded by the Gospels. Liberation theology demands that we put orthopraxis before orthodoxy. Gutiérrez calls this a 'preferential option for the poor' - God favours the poor, and so should the Church.

Exercise: What is orthopraxis and orthodoxy?

Exercise: Find at least three Biblical examples which show Jesus' favour towards the outcasts.

Juan Segundo taught that human dignity should be central to what we do – we are, after all, made in God's image. If we fail to intervene and advocate justice, we prove ourselves incompatible with biblical peace and justice. However, Segundo differed to Gutiérrez because he favoured spiritual liberation (from sin) before social liberation. The poor should, however, still be prioritised. John Paul II also highlighted an attention to spiritual poverty which can be caused by focusing too much on material wealth.

Exercise: Find out about Jesus' anointing at Bethany. How might this passage support Segundo's view?

The Catholic Church expressed concern about some of the theological use of Marx as he had some dangerous ideas. Evangelism was being threatened by the prospect of violent revolution and Cardinal Ratzinger taught that Christian liberation should focus on liberation from sin.

Exercise: Do you agree with Cardinal Ratzinger that Marxism is inherently un-Christian?

Thought Point

Bonaventure criticised liberation theology for prioritising action over the Gospel, equating theology with politics. The result is a side-lining of Christian evangelism. This emphasis on structural sin, Bonaventure said, would go against Jesus' emphasis on personal reconciliation with God.

Essay Skills

Types of questions

Questions on this topic might focus on the Marx's teaching on alienation and exploitation, on liberation theology's use of Marx to analyse social sin, or on liberation theology's teaching on the 'preferential option for the poor'. Whichever it asks, candidates should always use aspects of the other in evaluation. Some examples of questions you might be asked are these:

Q. To what extent should Christian theology engage with atheist secular ideologies?

A. Consider the strengths of Christianity's engagement with Marxism so far – successful?

- Consider Alastair Kee's view that liberation theology has been too conservative.

- Critically assess in light of criticisms that warn Christianity that it might lose its distinctiveness if it engages too much with atheist secular ideologies.

Q. "Liberation theology has not engaged with Marxism fully enough." Discuss.

A. Outline how liberation theology has engaged with Marxism and assess strengths and weakness of this involvement – social sin and preferential option for the poor. Consider José Miranda's view that Marxism is more relevant today.

Q. Critically assess the relationship of liberation theology and Marx with particular reference to liberation theology's use of Marx to analyse social sin.

A. Outline the relationship of liberation theology and Marx – e.g. to analyse the 'structural' aspects of social sin. How great an influence do you think Marxism had on this developing ideology or should it have naturally arisen out of the Gospel message? Consider the relative strengths of liberation theology and Marxism in tackling social issues and whether or not Christianity has engaged with Marxism enough. A question with a huge scope.

Exercise: Analyse this question: 'To what extent has liberation theology sufficiently engaged with Marxism?

Essay Skills – Introductions and Thesis Statement

Your introduction should:

1. indicate to the reader that you know what the question is about;

2. demonstrate the parameters of the question giving a sense of the two main sides of the argument

3. make clear where the essay will go, giving a clear thesis statement.

Exercise: Take this question: 'It is right for Christianity to prioritise one group over another.' Discuss.

Write an introduction making all three parts of the introduction clear and distinct. One sentence is enough for each, but make sure each sentence is clear and concise.

1. Definition and context: Identify what the question is about and the position of those in favour e.g. God favours the poor.

2. Parameters and opposition: State the opposing position, the position of some who would say Jesus' message of salvation is for all (the inclusivist view).

---

3. Thesis statement: Make it clear where you stand, with yes, no, or somewhere between. Be concise, outlining what your position is.

About the Authors

Daniella Dunsmore trained in Theology at Cambridge University. She is currently subject leader in Religious Studies at Thetford Grammar School, speaks at Conferences, and is a Teach First Ambassador.

Peter Baron is a highly experienced author, teacher and trainer. He is managing editor of the peped website.

To join the community please register your interest by filling in your details on the form on the website. We welcome contributions and suggestions so that our community continues to flourish and expand. Tutors are also available to help students taking or retaking the exam to achieve a top grade.

www.peped.org contains **EXTRACTS** and **FURTHER READING** mentioned in the exam specification, plus additional articles, handouts and essay plans. Notice that the exam specification merely gives guidance as to further reading - you may use any source or philosopher you find relevant to the construction of your argument. Indeed, if you have the courage to abandon the selection (and any examples) introduced by your textbook, you will relieve the examiner of boredom and arguably launch yourself on an A grade trajectory.

peterbaron@peped.org

Links, reviews, news and revision materials available on www.peped.org

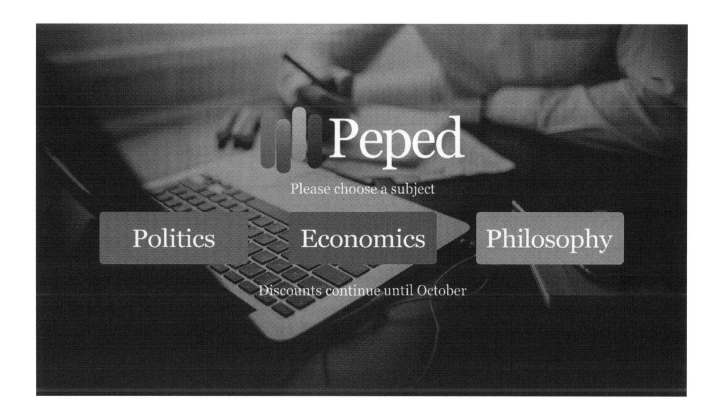

www.peped.org website allows students and teachers to explore Philosophy of Religion and Ethics through handouts, film clips, presentations, case studies, extracts, games and academic articles.

Pitched just right, and so much more than a text book, here is a place to engage with critical reflection whatever your level. Marked student essays are also posted.

Published by Active Education

www.peped.org

First published in 2018

ISBN: 9781717833976

Cartoons used with permission © Becky Dyer

All images © their respective owners